Jokes!
Jokes!!
Jokes!!!

'The four funniest books
in the history of the world.
I should know – I wrote them!'
Gyles Brandreth

First published by Madcap Books in 1997 as CRAZY JOKES, CRAZY PRACTICAL JOKES and CRAZY WORLD RECORDS.

This bumper edition first published in 1998 as JOKES! JOKES! JOKES! by Madcap Books, André Deutsch Ltd, 76 Dean Street, London W1V 5HA. André Deutsch Ltd is a subsidiary of VCI plc.
www.vci.co.uk

A catalogue record for this title is available from the British Library.

ISBN 0 233 99583 8

Printed by Mackays of Chatham.

Jokes!
Jokes!!
Jokes!!!

Gyles Brandreth

Illustrated by
Robert Nixon
Graham Thompson John Smyth
Mike Miller

Other books available from Madcap:

Crazy Crosswords
Crazy Graffiti
Crazy Hoaxes
Crazy Howlers
Crazy Inventions
Crazy Riddles
Crazy Spy File
Crazy Tongue Twisters
Crazy Words
The Knockout Knock-Knock Joke Book
The Madcap Giant Book of Jokes
The Rotten Eggs Joke Book
The Teddy Bear Joke Book
A Trunk Full of Laughs

Welcome!

Here they are: the four funniest books in the history of the world. The first three are full of jokes, jokes, jokes. The fourth is full of crazy records – and that's no joke...

Contents

THE DICTIONARY OF JOKES
RN.

Acoustics
The acoustics in this theatre are fantastic.
Pardon?

Admiral
What's higher than an admiral?
His hat.

Aircraft
What is big, hairy and flies to New York at 2250 kph?
King Kongcorde.

Ancestors
One of my ancestors died at Waterloo.
Really? Which platform?

Anger
FIRST MAN: *Why are you so angry?*
SECOND MAN: Oh, it's all the rage now.

Animals
TEACHER: *Name four animals of the cat family.*
PUPIL: Father cat, Mother cat, and two kittens.

Apples
TEACHER: *If I had forty apples in one hand and fifty in the other, what would I have?*
PUPIL: Big hands.

Archaeologist
What's the definition of an archaeologist?
A man whose career is in ruins.

Ark
What's the difference between Noah's Ark and Joan of Arc?
One was made of wood, and the other was Maid of Orleans.

Astronaut
What did the astronaut see in his frying-pan?
An unidentified frying object.

Astronauts
Where do astronauts leave their spaceships?
At parking meteors.

Athletics
What is the best diet for athletes?
Runner beans.

Atlantic
What do you get if you cross the Atlantic with the Titanic?
Halfway.

Attention
TEACHER: *I wish you'd pay a little attention.*
PUPIL: I'm paying as little as I can.

Audience
What's the difference between an angry audience and a cow with laryngitis?
One boos madly and the other moos badly.

Baby
How do you get a baby astronaut to sleep?
You rock-et.

Bad luck
When is it bad luck to have a black cat follow you?
When you are a mouse.

Baldness
Why is a bald man's head like Alaska?
It's a great white bear place.

Banana
What do you do if you find a blue banana?
Try to cheer it up.

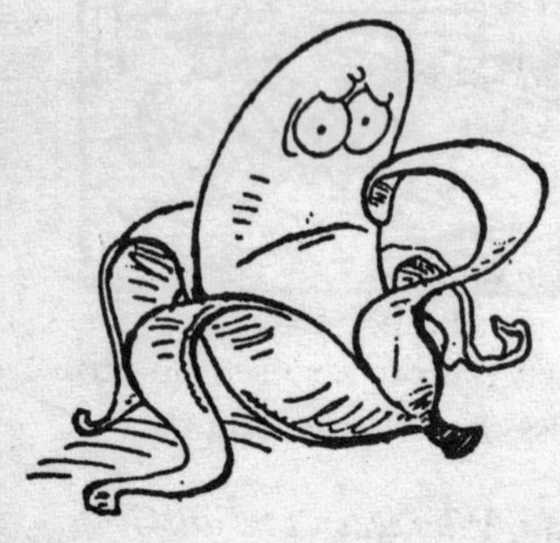

Band
CUSTOMER: *Will the band play anything I request?*
WAITER: Certainly sir.
CUSTOMER: *Tell them to play cards.*

Barber
BARBER: *Were you wearing a red scarf when you came in?*
CUSTOMER: No.
BARBER: *Oh! Then I must have cut your throat.*

Bath
Why did the bank robber take a bath?
So he could make a clean getaway.

Bears
Why do bears have fur coats?
Because they would look stupid in plastic macs.

Beaver
What did the beaver say to the tree?
It was nice gnawing you.

Bed
Why do people go to bed?
Because the bed won't come to them.

Bed
Shall I tell you the joke about the bed?
No, it hasn't been made yet.

Beehive
Why is a beehive like a rotten potato?
A beehive is a bee-holder, and a beholder is a spectator, and a specked tater is a rotten potato.

Beer
A barrel of beer fell on a man. Why wasn't he hurt?
It was light ale.

Bees
Why do bees hum?
Because they don't know the words.

Bell
What did the bell say when it fell in the water?
I'm wringing wet.

Birthday presents
What's the best birthday present?
Difficult question, but a drum takes a lot of beating.

Bison
What is the difference between a buffalo and a bison?
You can't wash your hands in a buffalo.

Bite
How do you find out where a flea has bitten you?
Start from scratch.

Blacksmith
The judge found the blacksmith guilty of forging.

Boating
Come in, Number 9. Your time is up.
But we've only got eight boats.
Are you in trouble, Number 6?

Bongos
INTERVIEWER: *Excuse my asking, but what are those tiny little bongos hanging from your ears?*
PUNK-STAR: Oh, they're just my ear-drums.

Bow
What kind of bow is impossible to tie?
A rainbow.

Brain
What's the cure for water on the brain?
A tap on the head.

Breakfast
What do ghosts have for breakfast?
Dreaded Wheat.

Broom
Why does a witch ride on a broom?
A vacuum cleaner is too heavy.

Brother
My brother thinks he's a chicken. We'd take him to the doctor but we can't do without the eggs.

Budgerigars
What is the best time to buy budgies?
When they are going cheap.

Bull
What did the bull say to the cow?
When I fall in love it will be for heifer.

Burglar
What did the burglar say to the lady of the house when she caught him stealing her silver?
I am at your service, Ma'am.

Burial
Why didn't they bury the Duke of Wellington with full military honours in 1847?
Because he didn't die until 1852.

Butcher

WOMAN: *I want a nice piece of bacon. And make it lean.*
BUTCHER: Which way, madam?

Butterfly

Why couldn't the butterfly get into the dance?
Because it was a moth-ball.

Cabbages

There were two parallel lines of cabbages, so the farmer called it a dual cabbage way.

Cakes

What jumps from cake to cake and tastes of almonds?
Tarzipan.

Candles

Candles make light meals.

Cannibal

Do you like beans?
Yes, very much.
What sort do you like eating best?
Human bein's.

Car
I recently bought a baby car – it doesn't go anywhere without a rattle.

Cards
Why is it dangerous to play cards in the jungle?
Because of all the cheetahs.

Cats
What do cats read every morning?
Mewspapers.

Charge
POLICEMAN: *I'm afraid that I'm going to have to lock you up for the night.*
MAN: What's the charge?
POLICEMAN: *Oh, there's no charge. It's all part of the service.*

Chemist
CUSTOMER: *Chemist, I'd like some poison for mice.*
CHEMIST: Have you tried Boots?
CUSTOMER: *I want to poison them – not kick them to death.*

Chess
My dog plays chess with me.
That's amazing! It must be a really intelligent animal.
Not really. I've won three games to two so far this evening.

Chickens
Who tells chicken jokes?
Comedihens.

Children
What children live in the sea?
Buoys and gulls.

Chops
CUSTOMER: *Waiter! This chop is very tough.*
WAITER: Yes sir, it's probably a karate chop.
CUSTOMER: *Well, have you got pig's trotters?*
WAITER: No, sir – flat feet.

Cinema
CINEMA ATTENDANT: *That's the sixth ticket you've bought.*
CUSTOMER: Yes, I know, there's a girl in there that keeps tearing them up.

Circle
Why were seven wooden planks standing in a circle?
They were having a board meeting.

Citrus fruits
How do you help deaf citrus fruits?
Give them a lemon aid.

Cleaning
Why did the cleaning woman stop cleaning?
Because she found grime doesn't pay.

Cobbler
What did the cobbler say when a flock of chickens came into his workshop?
Shoo!

Cock-a-doodle-do
What is the opposite of Cock-a-doodle-do?
Cock-a-doodle-don't.

Coffee
CUSTOMER: *Waiter! This coffee tastes like mud.*
WAITER: Well, sir, it was ground only ten minutes ago.

Containers
Can an orange box?
No, but a tomato can.

Cooks
Why are cooks cruel?
They beat eggs, whip cream and batter fish.

Cow
I say, what a lovely colour that cow over there is.
It's a Jersey.
Really? I thought it was her skin.

Cowboy
Who has eight guns and terrorises the ocean?
Billy the Squid.

Cowboys
FIRST COWBOY: *Did you know they call you 'Paleface' on the reservation?*
SECOND COWBOY: No – why's that?
FIRST COWBOY: *Because you've got a face like a bucket.*

Croak
What goes croak! croak! when it's misty?
A frog-horn.

Crocodile
What's a crocodile's favourite game?
Snap.

Cruelty
Why is a farmer cruel?
Because he pulls the corn by its ears.

Dancing
In one word, describe 154 dancing cakes.
Abundance.

Danger
What's green and highly dangerous?
A caterpillar with a machine gun.

December
What do you call a tug-of-war on December 24th?
Christmas 'Eave.

Dentist
MAN: *Give it me straight – how am I?*
DENTIST: Well, sir your teeth are all right – but I'm afraid your gums will have to come out.

Detective
What did the detective say when he tracked down the crook?
I'm policed to meet you.

Directions
MOTORIST: *Could you tell me the way to Bath?*
POLICEMAN: I always use soap and water.

Doctor

Why was the unemployed doctor angry?

Because he had no patients.

Dog

I've just lost my dog.

Why don't you put an advertisement in the paper?

Don't be silly – my dog can't read.

Dolphins

Dolphins are so intelligent that within only a few weeks of being in captivity they can train a man to stand on the very edge of their pool and throw them fish three times a day.

Doorbell

How do you use an Egyptian doorbell?

Toot-and-come-in.

Door knockers

What did they give the man who invented door knockers?

The No Bell Prize.

Dracula

Where is Dracula's office in America?

In the Vampire State Building.

Dress

CUSTOMER: *I would like to try on that dress in the window, please.*

ASSISTANT: I'm sorry, madam, you'll have to try it on in the changing-rooms like everybody else.

Ducks
What happens to ducks who fly upside down?
They quack up.

Dying
Why is a dying man like a cobbler?
Because he gives up his awl, looks to his end, and prepares his soul for the last.

Eggs
Have you heard the joke about the eggs?
No.
Two bad.

Elastic
Why is elastic one of the longest words in the dictionary?
Because it stretches.

Elections
What bird will never vote in an election?
A mynah bird, because he's too young.

Electrician
Why did the man become an electrician?
He was looking for a bit of light relief.

Electrician
What did the electrician's wife say when he arrived home late?
Wire you insulate?

Emergency
What happens when you dial 666?
A policeman comes along walking on his hands.

Eskimo

What do you call an Eskimo wearing five balaclavas?

Anything you like, because he can't hear you.

Excuses

TEACHER (on phone): *You say Johnny has a cold and can't come to school. To whom am I speaking?*

VOICE: This is my father.

Eye

JOE: *The police are looking for a man with one eye called Oscar McTavish.*

JIM: Oh, yes. And what's his other eye called?

Famous last words

At the inquest, the coroner gently asked the widow: 'Could you tell us what your late husband's last words were?'

'Yes,' she replied. 'He said: "I really don't see how they can make a profit out of selling this corned beef at ten pence a tin..."'

Fire

Who invented fire?

Oh, some bright spark.

Fireplace
Who invented the first fireplace?
Alfred the Grate.

Fir trees
What do sad fir trees do?
They pine a lot.

Fishermen
What is essential for deaf fishermen?
A herring aid.

Fjord
What is a Fjord?
A Norwegian motor car.

Fleas
How do you start a flea race?
One, two, flea . . . go!

Flowers
What did the big flower say to the little flower?
How are you, bud?

Flying squad
LADY TO POLICEMAN: Send for the flying squad, please, I've lost my canary.

France
What is French, 305 metres high and wobbly?
The Trifle Tower.

Free speech
Do you believe in free speech?
I certainly do.
Good, can I use your telephone?

Frog
What's a frog's favourite sweet?
A lollihop.

Frogs' legs
CUSTOMER: *Waiter, have you got frogs' legs?*
WAITER: No, sir, I always walk this way.

Garden
WOMAN: *You've been working in your garden for hours, what are you growing?*
GARDENER: Tired.

Geography
TEACHER: *Where are the Andes?*
PUPIL: At the end of my armies.

Geologists
Where do geologists put their samples?
In the rock-sacks.

Germs
Did you know that deep breathing kills germs?
Yes, but how do you get them to breathe deeply?

Giraffe
What do you get if you cross a giraffe with a dog?
An animal that barks at low-flying aircraft.

Gnomes
What do you feed under-nourished gnomes?
Elf-raising flour.

Gold
How do you make gold soup?
Put fourteen carrots in it.

Hair
Why do bees have sticky hair?
Because they have honey combs.

Hair
PATIENT: *My hair keeps falling out. Can you suggest anything to keep it in?*
DOCTOR: How about a carrier bag?

Hat
What did the hat say to the scarf?
You hang around while I go on ahead.

Hatstand
Why did the hatstand in the hall?
Because it had nowhere to sit.

Haute cuisine
MAN: *Waiter, can I have some horrible, greasy chips, an underdone egg, and a steak that tastes like an old boot?*
WAITER: I'm sorry, sir, but we couldn't possibly give you anything like that.
MAN: *Why not? That's what you gave me yesterday.*

Help
What sits in a fruit bowl and shouts for help?
A damson in distress.

Horse
What horse can't you ride?
A clothes horse.

Horse
Why has a horse got six legs?
Because he has forelegs in front and two legs behind.

Hotel

HOTEL MANAGER: *Well, sir, did you enjoy your stay here with us?*

GUEST: Yes, but I'm a bit upset about leaving the place so soon after I've practically bought it.

I

TEACHER: *Sue, say something beginning with 'I'.*

SUE: I is . . .

TEACHER: *No, Sue, you must say I am.*

SUE: All right, I am the ninth letter of the alphabet.

Igloo

What is an igloo?

An icicle made for two.

Illegal

What is meant by 'illegal'?

A sick bird of prey.

Jelly

What do you get when you cross a jelly with a sheep dog?

Collie-wobbles.

Jockey

Why did the jockey take hay to bed?

To feed his nightmares.

Judge

JUDGE: *Constable, do you recognise this woman?*

CONSTABLE: Yes, m'lud. She came up to me when I was in plain clothes and tried to pass this five-pound note off on me.

JUDGE: *Counterfeit?*

CONSTABLE: Yes, m'lud. She had two.

Judge
The judge was only four feet three inches tall – a small thing sent to try us.

Jungle
Why did an egg go into the jungle?
Because it was an eggsplorer.

Kangaroo
An Australian farmer tried to cross a kangaroo with a sheep so he would get a woolly jumper.

Killing
Could you kill somebody just by throwing eggs at him?
Yes, he would be eggs-terminated.

Kitchen
DINER: *This restaurant must have a very clean kitchen.*
WAITER: Thank you, sir, but how did you know?
DINER: *Everything tastes of soap.*

Lemon
What do you give a hurt lemon?
Lemonade, of course.

Lettuce
What's the difference between a mouldy lettuce and a dismal song?
One's bad salad and the other's a sad ballad.

Lies
I can't stop telling lies.
I don't believe you.

Lift
What did one lift say to the other lift?
I think I'm going down with something.

Light bulb
What would you do if you swallowed a light bulb?
Use a candle.

Lightning
Why does lightning shock people?
Because it doesn't know how to conduct itself.

Lobster
Why did the lobster blush?
Because the sea weed.

Madness
What do you call mad fleas?
Loony ticks.

Magician
What do you call a space magician?
A flying saucerer.

Mathematics
If two's company and three's a crowd, what is four and five?
Nine.

Meanness
Who is the meanest man in the world?
The man who finds a crutch, then breaks his leg so that he can use it.

Meat
WAITER: *And how did you find the meat, sir?*
CUSTOMER: Oh, I just lifted up a chip and there it was.

Medicine
DOCTOR: *Did you drink your medicine after your bath?*
PATIENT: After drinking the bath I didn't have too much room for the medicine.

Memory
PATIENT: *Doctor, Doctor, I've lost my memory.*
DOCTOR: When did this happen?
PATIENT: *When did what happen?*

Metal
Did you hear about the man who ate little bits of metal all day?
It was his staple diet.

Metronome
What is a metronome?
A dwarf in the Paris underground.

Minimum
What's the definition of minimum?
A very small mother.

Moses
How do we know that Moses wore a wig?
Because sometimes he was seen with Aaron and sometimes without.

Motherhood

A very proud mother phoned up a big Sunday newspaper and reported that she'd given birth to seventeen children. The girl at the desk didn't quite catch the message and asked: 'Would you repeat that?'

'Not if I can help it,' the woman replied.

Mouse

What is the largest species of mouse in the world?
A hippopotamouse.

Musician

Did you hear about the musician who spent all his time in bed?
Yes, he wrote sheet music.

Nailbiting

MAN: *At last I've cured my son of biting his nails.*
FRIEND: Really? How did you manage that?
MAN: *I knocked all his teeth out.*

Nationality

What nationality are you?
Well, my mother was born in Iceland and my father was born in Cuba so I suppose that makes me an ice cube.

Newsagent

Have you heard the one about the man who bought a paper shop? It blew away.

Nightwatchman

What's the difference between a nightwatchman and a butcher?
One stays awake and the other weighs a steak.

Noah's Ark

Why didn't the two worms go into Noah's ark in an apple?

Because everyone had to go in pairs.

Nuts

WOMAN IN A GREENGROCER'S: One pound of mixed nuts and not too many coconuts, please.

Octopus

What do you call a neurotic octopus?

A crazy, mixed-up squid.

Oil

Which animals have to be oiled?

Mice, because they squeak.

Oranges

An orange went to telephone a friend but the other orange didn't give her the message. Why?

Because the pips went.

Owl

What did the owl and the goat do at the square dance?

The hootenanny.

Oxygen
TEACHER: *If we breathe oxygen in the daytime, what do we breathe at night?*
PUPIL: Nitrogen?

Paint
PSYCHIATRIST: *And what seems to be the trouble?*
PATIENT: Well, doctor, I keep having this tremendous urge to paint myself all over with gold paint.
PSYCHIATRIST: *You are suffering from a gilt complex.*

Painting
What did the oil painting say to the wall?
First they framed me, then they hung me.

Pancakes
CUSTOMER: *Waiter, will the pancakes be long?*
WAITER: No, sir, round.

Party
How would you describe a party at a camping site?
Intense excitement.

Peach
DRINKER: *Excuse me, do you know how to make a fresh peach punch?*
BARMAN: Sure – give her boxing lessons.

Pen
PATIENT: *Doctor, Doctor, what can I do? My little boy has swallowed my pen.*
DOCTOR: Use a pencil till I get there.

Pencil
Shall I tell you the joke about the pencil?
No, there's no point in it.

Piano
PIANO TUNER: *I've come to tune your piano.*
MAN: But we didn't send for you.
TUNER: *No, but your neighbours did.*

Piglets
Why didn't the piglets listen to their father?
Because he was such a boar.

Pigs
What do you call a stupid pig thief?
A hamburglar.

Plumber
What vegetable needs a plumber?
A leek.

Pocket calculator
Would you like to buy a pocket calculator, sir?
No thanks, I know how many pockets I've got.

Police
What did the policeman say to the man with three heads?
"Allo, 'allo, 'allo.'

Pony
What do you give a pony with a cold?
Cough stirrup.

Pound note
PATIENT: *Doctor, Doctor, I feel like a £5 note.*
DOCTOR: Go shopping – the change will do you good.

Prisoners
NEWSCASTER: Two prisoners escaped today. One is seven feet tall and the other is four feet six inches. Police are looking high and low for them.

Pudding
How do you start a milk pudding race?
Sago.

Punctuality
TEACHER: *You should have been here at nine o'clock.*
PUPIL: Why, what happened?

Puppetry
What's the best way to get into the puppetry business?
Pull a few strings.

Putt
What goes putt-putt-putt-putt?
A bad golfer.

Questions
What never asks questions but gets plenty of answers?
A doorbell.

Rain
It's raining cats and dogs today.
I know – I've just stepped into a poodle.

Reindeer
What do reindeer say before they tell you a joke?
This one will sleigh you.

Road
Why did the elephant cross the road?
Because it was the chicken's day off.

Robbery
What sort of robbery is the easiest?
A safe robbery.

Robin Hood
What did Little John say when Robin Hood fired at him?
That was an arrow escape.

Rock cakes
What do you do if somebody offers you a rock cake?
Take your pick.

Romance
'Darling, do you love me?' sighed Romeo.
'Of course I do,' sighed Juliet.
'Darling, whisper something soft and sweet in my ear.'
'Lemon meringue pie.'

Runner
Who was the fastest runner in history?
Adam. He was the first in the human race.

Sandwiches
What did the traffic warden have in his sandwiches?
Traffic jam.

Sausages
PATIENT: *Doctor, my family think I'm mad.*
DOCTOR: Why?
PATIENT: *Because I like sausages.*
DOCTOR: Nonsense, I like sausages too.
PATIENT: *You do? You must come round and see my collection. I have hundreds.*

Sheep
A man goes into a butcher's shop and says, 'Have you got a sheep's head?'
The butcher replies, 'No, it's just the way I part my hair.'

Sheep
PATIENT: *Doctor, I've just swallowed a sheep.*

DOCTOR: How do you feel?
PATIENT: *Very ba-a-a-ad.*

Shoes
What wears shoes, but has no feet?
The pavement.

Sleep
PATIENT: *Doctor, Doctor, I can't get to sleep at night.*
DOCTOR: Lie on the edge of the bed and you'll soon drop off.

Soccer
CAPTAIN: *Why didn't you stop the ball?*
GOALIE: What do you think the nets are for?

Soup
CUSTOMER: *Waiter, what soup is this?*
WAITER: It's bean soup, sir.
CUSTOMER: *I don't care what it was, I want to know what it is now.*

Spaceman
What do you call a crazy spaceman?
An astronut.

Spectacles
DOCTOR: *You need glasses.*
PATIENT: How did you know?
DOCTOR: *I could tell as soon as you walked through the window.*

Spelling
How do you spell 'Crocodile'?
K-r-o-k-o-d-i-a-l.
The dictionary spells it 'C-r-o-c-o-d-i-l-e.'
You didn't ask me how the dictionary spelt it.

Spies
What is the most common illness among spies?
A code in the nose.

Splinters
From which seafaring book can you get splinters?
A log-book.

Spoon
PATIENT: *Doctor, Doctor, I feel like a spoon.*
DOCTOR: Sit down and don't stir.

Spy
What do you call a frog spy?
A croak and dagger agent.

Stories
What do you call a pig who tells long, dull stories?
A big boar.

Streets
When are the streets most greasy?
When the rain is dripping.

Stupidity
What makes you think I'm so stupid?
Well, when you went to that mind-reader, she only charged you half-price!

Sty
What do you call pigs who live together?
Pen friends.

Suit
I've just bought a suit that fits me like a glove – four trouser legs and one sleeve.

Sunglasses
Have you heard the one about the man who always wore sunglasses? He took a dim view of things.

Supper
What did the cannibal have for supper?
Baked beings on toast.

Swiss roll
How do you make a Swiss roll?
Push him off the top of an alp.

Teeth
What's got teeth but can't bite?
A comb.

Telegram
Why is it useless to send a telegram to Washington?
Because he's dead.

Theatre
Why is the theatre such a sad place?
The seats are always in tiers.

Time
How can you check the time without looking at your watch?
Eat an apple and count the pips.

Tin-openers
What dance do tin-openers do?
The Can-Can.

Tonsils
FIRST TONSIL: *What are you getting dressed up for?*
SECOND TONSIL: Oh, the doctor is taking me out tonight.

Tooth
How do you get through life with only one tooth?
You grin and bare it.

Tower of Pisa
What makes the Tower of Pisa lean?
A strict diet.

Traffic lights
What did the traffic lights say to the sports car?
Don't look now, I'm changing.

Train driver
What's the difference between a train driver and a teacher?
One minds the train and the other trains the mind.

Travel
How long is the next bus?
Oh, about six metres.

Twig
CUSTOMER: *Waiter, there's a twig in my soup.*
WAITER: Hold on, sir, I'll call the branch manager.

Twins
What language do twins speak in Holland?
Double Dutch.

Umbrella
When should a mouse carry an umbrella?
When it's raining cats and dogs.

Vampires
What dance do vampires do?
The Fangdango.

Vegetarian
Why did the cannibal become a vegetarian?
Well, you can go off people, you know.

Vikings
What did Vikings use for secret messages?
The Norse Code.

Volcano
What's the definition of a volcano?
A mountain with a hiccup.

Volkswagens
Where do Volkswagens go when they get old?
The Old Volks Home.

Waiter
CUSTOMER: *There's only one piece of meat on my plate.*
WAITER: Wait a minute, sir, and I'll cut it in two.

Watch
What does your watch say?
'Tick, tock!'

Water
When is water musical?
When it's piping hot.

Water otter
What is the proper name for a water otter?
A kettle.

Week
Who invented the five-day-week?
Robinson Crusoe. He had all his work done by Friday.

Weight
What's a good way of putting on weight?
Eat a peach, swallow the centre, and you've gained a stone.

Whales
Where do you weigh whales?
At a whale weigh station.

Window
Why did a man throw his watch out of the window?
To see time fly.

Witch

What is the difference between a very small witch and a deer running from the hunter?

One is a stunted hag and the other a hunted stag.

Woodpecker

What do you get when you cross a carrier pigeon with a woodpecker?

A bird who knocks before he delivers his message.

Wool

What happened to the cat that ate a ball of wool?

It had mittens.

Worm

How can you tell which end of the worm is his head?

Tickle his middle and see which end smiles.

Yellow

What's yellow on the inside and green on the outside?

A banana disguised as a cucumber.

Zebra

What do you get if you cross a zebra with a pig?

Striped sausages.

Zebra crossing

POLICEMAN TO PEDESTRIAN: *Here! Why are you crossing the road in this dangerous spot – can't you see there's a zebra crossing only fifty yards away?*

PEDESTRIAN: Well, I hope it's having better luck than I am.

THE JOKE
DICTIONARY

Animal Magic

FARMER: *What is the treatment for a pig with a sore throat?*
VET: You must apply this oinkment.

MOTHER: *Jane, have you given the goldfish fresh water today?*
JANE: No. They haven't finished what I gave them yesterday.

What did the croaking frog say to his friend?
I think I've got a person in my throat!

What would you get if you crossed a flea with a rabbit?
A bug's bunny.

JACK: *If your dog was chewing up your favourite book, what would you do?*
JILL: I'd take the words right out of his mouth.

How does an octopus go into battle?
Well armed!

JIM: *How is a skunk different from a rabbit?*
JOE: I don't know. How?
JIM: *The skunk uses a cheaper deodorant!*

Mrs Barker went along to the Battersea Dogs' Home to get a dog as a present for her little boy.

'Are you sure this mongrel will make a good pet?' she asked the keeper.

'Without a doubt, madam,' said the keeper. 'He'll make a wonderful pet. He'll eat anything and he's especially fond of children.'

BLACK SHEEP: *Baa-a-a-a-a-a.*
WHITE SHEEP: Moo!
BLACK SHEEP: *What do you mean, 'Moo'?*
WHITE SHEEP: I'm learning a foreign language.

What should you do if you wake up in the middle of the night and hear a mouse squeaking?
Oil it!

BILL: *What kind of dog is that?*
BEN: He's a police dog.
BILL: *He doesn't look much like a police dog to me.*
BEN: Of course not: he's a plain clothes police dog!

LITTLE BOY BLUE: *Baa, baa, black sheep, have you any wool?*
BLACK SHEEP: What do you think this is, you nitwit, nylon?

DICK: *Tom has been sent to prison for stealing a pig.*
HARRY: How could they prove that he did it?
DICK: *The pig squealed!*

If you feed a cow £5 notes what will you get?
Rich milk.

A man went to an animal auction not long ago and found just what he wanted. It was a beautiful African parrot and the man decided to bid for it. The bids went higher and higher, but finally the man managed to get the bird for £699, the highest price ever paid for an African parrot in an animal auction. As soon as he had bought the bird, the man suddenly remembered that he had forgotten to find out the most important thing about the parrot.

'Does the parrot talk?' he asked the auctioneer anxiously.

'Who do you think was bidding against you all the time?' was the auctioneer's reply.

Best-sellers

According to the latest figures supplied by bookshops throughout the world, these are the twenty best-selling titles of all time:

1 The Greatest Detective Stories Ever by *Watts E. Dunn*
2 Silence is Golden *by Xavier Breth*
3 How I Won the Pools *by Jack Potts*
4 Parachute Jumping *by Hugo Furst*
5 How Not to Shoot Your Wife *by Mr Completely*
6 The Joys of Hitchhiking *by Marsha Long*
7 What's Up, Doc? *by Howie Dewin*
8 Who Killed Cock Robin? *by Howard I. Know*
9 The Art of Button-Collecting *by Zipporah Broaken*
10 How to Fall Out of the Window *by Eileen Dover*
11 Why You Need Insurance *by Justin Case*
12 Monster-Making as a Hobby *by Frank N. Stine*
13 My Life in a Lunatic Asylum *by I. M. Nutty*
14 Around the Mountain *by Sheila B. Cumming*
15 Peek-a-Boo *by I. C. Hugh*

16 Neck Exercise *by G. Rarff*
17 How to Make an Igloo *by S. K. Mow*
18 Outsize Clothes *by L. E. Fant*
19 How to Diet *by M. T. Cupboard*
20 The Pleasures of Horse-Riding *by Jim Karna*

Cross-Breeding

What do you get if you cross a round black hat with a rocket?

A very fast bowler.

What do you get if you cross a miserable man with a spaceship?

A moan-rocket.

What do you get if you cross a group of stars with a silver cup?

A constellation prize.

What do you get if you cross a space pistol, a cheer, and a hippopotamus?

A hip-hippo-ray gun.

What do you get if you cross the Moon with the top of a house?

A lun-attic.

What do you get if you cross two parts of the head, one treble-o, and Attila.

Ear-tooth-thousand and Hun (year 2001).

Daffinitions

Accord A thick piece of string

Acorn Something caused by a tight shoe

Address Something worn by girls and women

Adore Entrance to a house

Alphabet soup Eating your own words

Bachelor A man who never Mrs anyone

Bandleader Someone who has to face the music

Bathing beauty A girl worth wading for

Bird house Home tweet home

Blockhead A person who gets splinters every time he scratches his head

Cannibal A person who is fed up with people

Castor oil A lubricant for fishing rods

Celery What you get for working

Coconut Someone who is crazy about hot chocolate

Conceit A case of 'I' strain

Denial The main river of Egypt

Diet A triumph of mind over platter

Divine What the grapes grow on

Drill Sergeant An army dentist

Dumbwaiter Someone who can't get your order right

Eclipse What a gardener does to a hedge

Engineers What engines hear with

Entrance Be in a deep hypnotic state

Everest The laziest mountain in the world

Explain Eggs cooked without any trimmings

Fireman Someone who ought to go to blazes

Fission An atomic scientist's favourite pastime

Flying saucer A dish that is out of this world

Foul language What you hear if you pass near the chicken coop

Free speech When you can use someone else's phone

Garden hose Socks worn while you work in the garden

Ghost writer A spooksman

Giraffe The highest form of animal life

Goose A bird that grows down as it grows up

Gross ignorance 144 times worse than ordinary ignorance

Half a loaf A short holiday

Half-wit Someone who spends half his time being funny

Hatchet What a hen does with an egg

Hollow An empty greeting

Horse doctor A physician with a sore throat

Ice Skid stuff

Ice cream Yell at the top of your voice

Icicle An eavesdropper

Illegal A sick bird

Indistinct Where you put the dirty dishes

Jack-in-the-box An open and shut case

Jargon A missing container

Jet-setter A fast-flying dog

Jitterbug A nervous insect

Jonah The strongest man in the Bible. Even a whale could not keep him down

Kidnap What a small child often does after lunch

Kindred An abnormal fear of relatives

Knob A thing to adore

Launch A meal for astronauts

Lazy bones A skeleton that doesn't like work

Leopard An animal easy to spot

Library The tallest building in the world because it has the most stories

Lisp When you call a spade a thpade

Mayor A female horse

Meow A catty remark

Mistake A woman shoplifter

Moonbeams What holds the moon up

Mushroom The place where they serve the school food

Nightingale Very windy evening

Nightmare A horse that keeps late hours

Noise A cause of earitation

Noodle soup Nourishment for the brain

Normalise Good vision

Occur A mongrel dog

Ohm There is no place like it

Open house Home without a roof

Ouch The sound heard when two porcupines kiss

Out-of-bounds An elderly kangaroo

Pasteurise Beyond what you can see

Peephole Members of the human race

Piano chord What you tie a piano up with

Pillow Headquarters

Playpen A writing device used by dramatists

Quack A doctor who treats sick ducks

Quadruplets Four crying out loud

Quartz There are four to a gallon

Ragtime When your clothes wear out

Refuse What must be done when all the lights in the house go out

Relief What trees do each spring

River bank Where fish keep their money

Robin A bird that steals

School spirit Ghost that haunts a school

Seashell A torpedo

Short cut A small wound

Snack A refresher course

Sourpuss A cat that has swallowed a lemon

Temper The only thing you can lose and still have

Tortoise What the teacher did

Treason The male offspring of a tree

Unaware What you put on first and take off last

Undercover agent A spy in bed

Underground garage A wall-to-wall car pit

Unit A term of abuse

Urchin The lower part of a woman's face

Vicious circle A round geometric figure with a nasty temper

Volcano A mountain that has blown its stack

Volga boatman A coarse seaman

Watchmaker Someone who works overtime

Wheeler dealer A car-tyre salesman

Witchcraft A flying broomstick

Woe The opposite of 'giddyup'

Wristwatch A clock for people who don't like time on their hands

X What hens lay

X-ray Bellyvision

Yank A dentist of American extraction

Yardstick Something that has three feet but can't walk

Yearnings What you receive for working

Zebra A horse with venetian blinds

Zing What you do with a zong

Zoo A place where people go and animals are barred

Epilaughs

These three epitaphs are taken from actual gravestones found in the United Kingdom:

'Here snug in grave my wife doth lie;
Now she's at rest and so am I!'

'Here lie the bones of Richard Lawton,
Whose death, alas! was strangely brought on.
Trying one day his corns to mow off,
The razor slipped and cut his toe off;
His toe, or rather what it grew to,
An inflammation quickly flew to,
Which took alas to mortifying,
And was the cause of Richard's dying.'

'Here lie I,
Bereft of breath,
Because a cough
Carried me off;
Then a coffin
They carried me off in.'

Family Fun

MOTHER: *Come in, Darren, and I'll give you some chocolate biscuits. Are your feet dirty?*
DARREN: Yes, Mum, but I've got my shoes on.

MOTHER: *You behaved very nicely in church today, dear.*
DAUGHTER: Yes, when that nice man offered me a whole plate of money I said, 'No, thank you.'

JACK: *My grandfather has a wooden leg.*
JILL: That's nothing, my grandmother has a cedar chest.

SON: *Dad, what is a weapon?*
DAD: It's something you fight with.
SON: *Is mother your weapon?*

HUSBAND: *My wife treats me like an idol.*
FRIEND: Why do you say that?
HUSBAND: *She feeds me burnt offerings at every meal.*

LITTLE WILLIE: *Mummy, do you remember that special plate you always worried I would break?*
MOTHER: Yes, what about it?
LITTLE WILLIE: *Well, your worries are over!*

A grandfather took his young grandson to the opera for the very first time as a special treat. The conductor began to wave his baton and the soprano started to sing her famous aria. The boy was fascinated by everything he saw and heard, but eventually he turned to his grandfather and asked, 'Why is he hitting her with his stick?'

'He's not hitting her,' answered the grandfather with a smile.

'Well, if he's not hitting her, why is she screaming?'

Little Willie rushed out of the bathroom. 'Oh, Mum,' he cried, 'I've just seen something running across the bathroom floor with no legs!'

'Nonsense, dear. What on earth are you talking about?'

'Water!'

Grub's up

Here's a glorious gaggle of gags for greedy guzzlers.

What did the fat man say when he sat down to eat his dinner?
I'm afraid this food is all going to waist.

JULIET: *May I have a fried egg?*
MOTHER: With pleasure.
JULIET: *No, with chips!*

MOTHER: *If you eat any more of that pie, you'll burst.*
LITTLE WILLIE: Okay, Mum – just pass the pie and get out of the way.

TOM: *Mum made an awful mistake today and gave Dad soap flakes instead of cornflakes for breakfast!*
DICK: Was he angry?
TOM: *He foamed at the mouth!*

MOTHER: *Eat your spinach, dear. It will put colour into your cheeks.*
JOHNNY: Who wants green cheeks?

Howlers

We all make mistakes. Among the most entertaining mistakes are the ones we make at school. Here are fifty classic schoolroom howlers to prove the point.

1 Antimony is money inherited from your mother's aunt.
2 Cosmic rays are electric treatment to make women beautiful.
3 Philatelists were a race of people who lived in Biblical times.
4 All people were petrified in the Stone Age.
5 Socrates died from an overdose of wedlock.
6 Austerity is an old religion but today even politicians teach it.
7 Blood consists of red corkscrews and white corkscrews.
8 Jacob had a brother called Seesaw.
9 Ladies who sing low kinds of songs are called contraltos.

10 A trombone is an instrument you play by pulling it in and out.
11 The Gorgons had long snakes in their hair. They looked like women only more horrible.
12 Poetry is when every line starts with a capital letter.
13 When a dog has puppies it is called a litre.
14 An oxygen has eight sides.
15 Euthanasia is the eastern part of Asia.
16 All Mormons are polygons.
17 The Merchant of Venice was a famous Italian who bought and sold canal boats.
18 When a man is married to one woman it is called monotony.
19 Kubla Khan is a black secret society wearing white night shirts.
20 Homer wrote *The Oddity*.
21 A convoy is a collection of small birds like cartridges.
22 Herrings go about the sea in shawls.
23 Reefs are what you put on coffins.
24 Pegasus is a hobby horse used by carpenters.
25 Soviet is another name for a table napkin.
26 Letters in sloping type are called hysterics.
27 A blizzard is the inside of a chicken.
28 A ruminating animal chews its cubs.
29 Mushrooms look like umbrellas because they grow where it's wet.

30 A centimetre is an insect with a hundred legs.
31 The future of 'I give' is 'You take'.
32 The vowels are: a, e, i, o, u, and sometimes w and y.
33 The passive verb is when the subject is the sufferer, as 'I am loved'.
34 A metaphor is a suppressed smile.
35 Water is composed of Oxygin and Hydrogin. Oxygin is pure but Hydrogin is gin and water.
36 There are four elements, mustard, salt, pepper and vinegar, although I think vinegar is really an acid.
37 A good cosmetic is salt and water. Cosmetics make you sick.
38 Handel was a little boy in a tale with his sister called *Handel and Grettal*.
39 Tom Sawyer was a smart boy, his character was always good sometimes.
40 The appendix is a part of the book for which nobody has found much use.
41 'The child is father to the man'. This was written by Shakespeare. He didn't often make that kind of mistake.
42 Marshal Goering was a fat man because he was one of Hitler's stoutest supporters.
43 Washington was a great general who always began a battle with the fixed determination to win or lose.
44 Dusk is little bits of fluff you find under the bed.
45 Necessity is the mother of convention.
46 A graven image is a nice gravestone.
47 Income is a yearly tax.
48 A surname is the name of somebody you say 'Sir' to.
49 Faith is believing what you know is untrue.
50 Ambiguity is telling the truth when you don't mean to.

It pays to advertise

Sign on a travel agency window:
PLEASE GO AWAY

Sign at a butcher's shop:
HONEST SCALES – NO TWO WEIGHS ABOUT IT

Sign outside a laundry:
WE'LL CLEAN FOR YOU, WE'LL PRESS FOR YOU, WE'LL EVEN DYE FOR YOU

Sign on a bird's cage in a pet shop:
FOR SALE – CHEEP

Sign outside a hotel:
WANTED – HOTEL WORKERS: ONLY INEXPERIENCED NEED APPLY

Sign at a tyre depot:
WE SKID YOU NOT

Sign outside a shoe shop:
COME IN AND HAVE A FIT

Sign outside a funeral directors:
SATISFACTION GUARANTEED OR YOUR MUMMY BACK

Joking on the job

FIRST GARDENER: *I used to work with thousands under me.*
SECOND GARDENER: Really?
FIRST GARDENER: *Yes, I cut the grass in a cemetery!*

TOM: *Did you hear about the angel who lost his job?*
DICK: No, what happened?
TOM: *He had harp failure.*

TIM: *My dad makes faces all day.*
TOM: Why does he do that?
TIM: *Because he works in a clock factory!*

The site foreman had ten very lazy labourers working for him, so he decided to try to trick them into doing some work.

'I've got a nice easy job today for the laziest man here,' he said. 'Will the laziest man please put up his hand.'

Nine hands went up.

'Why didn't you put your hand up?' he asked the tenth man.

'Too much trouble,' was the reply.

PRISONER: *The judge sent me here for the rest of my life.*
PRISON GOVERNOR: Got any complaints?
PRISONER: *Do you call breaking rocks with a hammer rest?*

What sort of children does a florist have?
Blooming idiots!

CHEF: *What is the best thing to put in a pie?*
TRAINEE: Your teeth!

CUSTOMER IN A HURRY: *Give me a mousetrap quickly, please. I've only two minutes to catch a train.*
SHOP ASSISTANT: Sorry, we don't have any that big!

JACK: *I hear the men are striking.*
JILL: What for?
JACK: *Shorter hours.*
JILL: Good for them. I've always thought sixty minutes was too long for an hour.

CONDUCTOR: *Will you please open the piano?*
PIANIST: I can't. The keys are on the inside!

JACK: *Did you hear what the burglar gave his wife for her birthday?*
JILL: No, what?
JACK: *A stole.*

Knock Knock knonsense

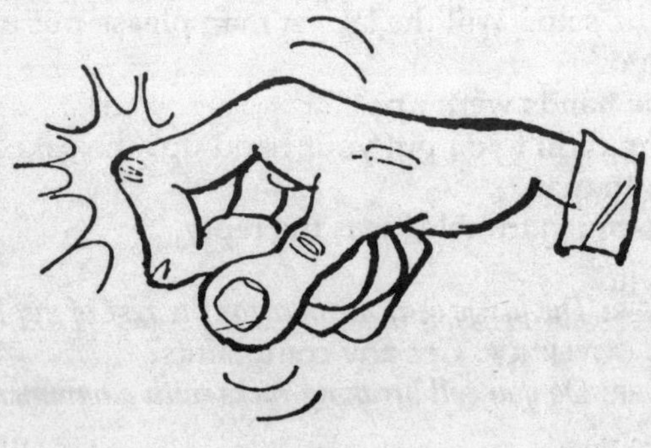

A
Knock Knock
Who's there?

Ammonia.
Ammonia who?
Ammonia a bird in a gilded cage.

B

Knock Knock
Who's there?
Barbara.
Barbara who?
'Barbara black sheep, have you any wool . . . ?'

C

Knock Knock
Who's there?
Cereal.
Cereal who?
Cereal pleasure to meet you.

D

Knock Knock
Who's there
Dawn.
Dawn who?
Dawn do anything I wouldn't do.

E

Knock Knock
Who's there?
Earl.
Earl who?
Earl be glad to tell you if you open the door.

F

Knock Knock
Who's there?
Felix.

Felix who?
Felix-cited all over.

G
Knock Knock
Who's there?
Guinevere.
Guinevere who?
Guinevere going to get together?

H
Knock Knock
Who's there?
Hiram.
Hiram who?
Hiram fine, how are you?

I
Knock Knock
Who's there?
Ina Claire.
Ina Claire who?
'Ina Claire day, you can see forever...'

J
Knock Knock
Who's there?
Joan.
Joan who?
Joan call us, we'll call you.

K
Knock Knock
Who's there?
Kent.
Kent who?
Kent you tell who it is?

L
Knock Knock
Who's there?
Lucy.
Lucy who?
Lucy lastic makes your pants fall down.

M
Knock Knock
Who's there?
Myth.
Myth who?
Myth you, too.

N
Knock Knock
Who's there?
Noah.
Noah who?
Noah don't know who you are either.

O
Knock Knock
Who's there?
Olive.
Olive who?
Olive you too, honey.

P
Knock Knock
Who's there?
Police.
Police who?
Police open the door.

Q
Knock Knock
Who's there?
Quebec.
Quebec who?
Quebec to the end of the line.

R
Knock Knock
Who's there?
Roland.
Roland who?
Roland stone gathers no moss.

S
Knock Knock
Who's there?
Sarah.
Sarah who?
Sarah doctor in the house?

T
Knock Knock
Who's there?
Tennis.
Tennis who?
Tennis five plus five.

U
Knock Knock
Who's there?
Utica.
Utica who?
Utica high road and I'll take the low road.

V
Knock Knock
Who's there?

Viola.
Viola who?
Viola sudden you don't know me?

W
Knock Knock
Who's there?
Wicked.
Wicked who?
Wicked make beautiful music together.

X
Knock Knock
Who's there?
Xavier.
Xavier who?
Xavier breath! I'm not leaving.

Y
Knock Knock
Who's there?
Yoga.
Yoga who?
Yoga what it takes!

Z
Knock Knock
Who's there?
Zaul.
Zaul who?
Zaul there is and there ain't no more.

Lear's limericks

Edward Lear died on 29th January 1888 at the age of 75, but his nonsense will live for ever. He didn't invent the limerick, but he made it world-famous. In his lifetime he wrote hundreds of limericks, and here are five firm favourites:

There was a Young Lady of Dorking,
Who bought a large bonnet for walking:
But its colour and size so bedazzled her eyes
That she very soon went back to Dorking.

There was an Old Man with a nose,
Who said, 'If you choose to suppose
That my nose is too long, you are certainly wrong!'
That remarkable Man with a nose.

There was a Young Lady whose nose
Was so long that it reached to her toes;
So she hired an Old Lady, whose conduct was steady,
To carry that wonderful nose.

There was an Old Man who said, 'Hush!
I perceive a young bird in this bush!'
When they said – 'Is it small?' He replied – 'Not at all!
It is four times as big as the bush!'

There was a Young Lady whose chin
Resembled the point of a pin;
So she had it made sharp, and purchased a harp,
And played several tunes with her chin.

Motoring madness

A motorist was driving down a one-way street the wrong way. He was stopped by a policeman on a motorbike.

POLICEMAN: *Do you know where you're going?*

DRIVER: Yes, but I must be very late. Everyone else is coming back!'

What kind of song do you sing in a car?
A cartoon!

What kind of driver never gets arrested?
A screwdriver.

What part of the car is the cause of most accidents?
The nut that holds the wheel!

What is an autobiography?
The life story of an automobile.

TOM: *People complain about backseat driver, but I have to say that I've been driving all my life and I've never heard a word from the back seat.*
DICK: What kind of car do you drive?
TOM: *A hearse!*

What age is most important?
Mileage!

GARAGE MECHANIC: *Is your horn broken?*
MOTORIST: No, it doesn't care.
GARAGE MECHANIC: *What do you mean?*
MOTORIST: It doesn't give a hoot!

Sign in a factory where they make mini cars:
THINK BIG – AND YOU'RE FIRED!

News flash

The marriage of the two lighthouse keepers was said last night to be on the rocks...

The Chancellor of the Exchequer announced today that under a new pay award scheme barbers are to get more fringe benefits...

Last night a large hole was made in the forty foot high fence surrounding the Broadstairs' Nudist Camp. Police are now looking into it...

Owing to a strike at the Meteorological Office, there will be no weather tomorrow...

The Common Market Commissioners' plan to have all meat pies wrapped in tin has been foiled...

Marmaduke Mustard, the recently elected Member

of Parliament for Puddlecombe, took his seat in the House of Commons this morning – but he was forced to put it back.

One hundred tonnes of human hair was stolen last night from a wig factory in Scunthorpe. Police are combing the area...

The Chairman of the British Periscope Manufacturers' Association said last night that business was looking up...

Odd ode

A boy who swims may say he swum,
But milk is skimmed and seldom skum,
And nails you trim, they are not trum.
When words you speak, these words are spoken,
But a nose is tweaked and can't be twoken,
And what you seek is seldom soken.
If we forget then we've forgotten,
But things we wet are never wotten,
And houses let cannot be lotten.
The goods one sells are always sold,

But fears dispelled are not dispold,
And what you smell is never smold.
When young, a top you oft saw spun,
But did you see a grin e'er grun,
Or a potato nearly skun?

Pun fun

INTERVIEWER: *Why have you called your new play 'The Broken Leg?'*
PLAYWRIGHT: Because it needs a strong cast!

ESTATE AGENT: *I have got the ideal house for you, sir. It really is perfect. It doesn't have a flaw.*
HOUSE BUYER: But what do you walk on?

Did you know that Prince Charles was a bit of a cry-baby when he was small? That's why they called him The Prince of Wails!

Did you hear about the bossy chicken that stopped on the railway track? She wanted to lay it on the line!

JACK: *My father can play the piano by ear.*
JILL: That's nothing! My father fiddles with his whiskers!

TOM: *Who was Snow White's brother?*
DICK: Egg White!
HARRY: *I don't get the yolk!*

What did the adding machine say to the cashier?
You can count on me!

TOM: *Tell me, Dick, why do you always sleep in that oil tank?*
DICK: Because I like to get up oily in the morning!

There were two buckets sitting in the kitchen cupboard chatting to one another.

'You don't look like a well bucket,' said one.

'You're quite right,' replied the other, 'I am a little pail!'

Quick questions

1 If a plug doesn't fit, do you socket?

2 Does fishing result in net profits?

3 Is a budget a baby budgerigar?

4 If you cross a cat with a ball of wool, will you get mittens?

5 Is the Lord Privy Seal a noble animal rather like a sealion who lives in a lavatory?

Ridiculous riddles

When the orange wanted to fight the banana, why did the banana run away?
Because it was yellow.

Which fish go to heaven when they die?
Angel fish.

What did the old man do when he thought he was dying?
He moved into the living room.

Where do butterflies go to dance?
Moth balls.

Why did the scientist take a ruler to bed?
To see how long he slept.

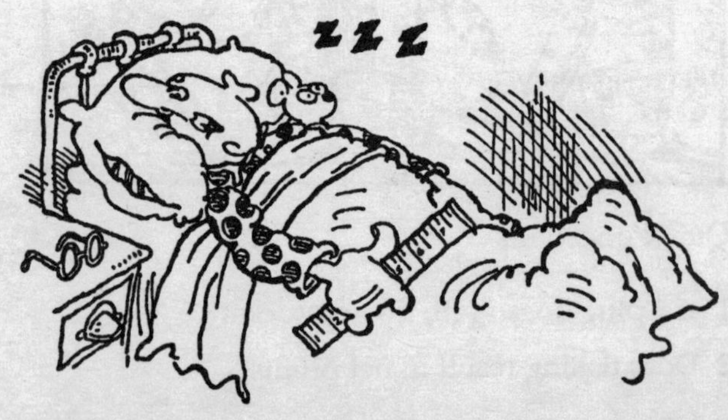

What do you call a baby whale that's crying?
A little blubber.

Why does a rooster watch TV?
For hentertainment.

Why did the hero refuse to die for his lady love?
Because his was an undying love.

How does one get on to something in which there's a lot of money?
Climb on to the roof of a bank.

Why are manicurists always so wealthy?
Because they make money hand over fist.

Why did the boy wear two suits to the fancy dress party?
He went as twins.

Why is a belt like a dustcart?
Because it goes round and gathers the waist.

What's more dangerous than being with a fool?
Fooling with a bee.

Why did the girl put her hands in the alphabet soup?
Because she was groping for words.

From a medical point of view, why is a pig unique?
Because you kill him before you cure him.

Why did the man have a high-pitched voice and funny teeth?
Because he had a falsetto voice and a false set o' teeth.

Why was the doctor who fell into a well a fool?
Because he should have attended the sick and left the well alone.

Why is a squeaky shoe a great composer?
Because it has music in its sole.

What is the cheapest way to get to China?
Be born there.

Why do white sheep eat more than black ones?
Because there are more white sheep in the world.

Why do we buy clothes?
Because we can't get them for nothing.

If a man smashed a clock, could he be accused of killing time?
Not if the clock struck first.

When is a shaggy dog most likely to enter your house?
When the door's open.

What is striped and goes round and round?
A zebra caught in a revolving door.

What is always behind time?
The back of a watch.

Why did the dishonest man grow a beard?
So no one could call him a bare-faced liar.

Which horses have their eyes nearest together?
The smallest horses.

Why can't a man marry his widow's sister?
Because he'd be dead.

How can you avoid falling hair?
Jump out of the way.

Why couldn't the boy sleep in class?
Because the teacher talked too loudly.

What would happen if you crossed a chicken with a poodle?
The chicken would lay pooched eggs.

What are the three nicest nuts in the world?
Walnuts, peanuts and forget-me-nuts.

What's the difference between a milkmaid and a seagull?
One skims milk and the other skims water.

How do you know that a sausage doesn't like being fried?
Because it spits.

What did the piece of wood say to the electric drill?
You bore me.

Why did the poor dog chase his own tail?
He was trying to make both ends meet.

Why was the sick boy about to croak?
Because he swallowed a frog.

How can you stop a rooster from crowing on Sunday?
Eat him on Saturday.

If you had fifteen cows and four goats, what would you have?
Plenty of milk.

Why was the farmer cross?
Someone had walked on his corn.

What can run and whistle – but can't walk or talk?
A locomotive.

What's the most intelligent insect you'll meet at school?
A spelling bee.

What falls but never gets hurt?
Snow.

Which takes less time to get ready for a trip: an elephant or a rooster?
A rooster, because he only takes his comb, while the elephant has to take a whole trunk.

What country is useful at mealtimes?
China.

Science spot

TOP SCIENTIST: *What does HNO_3 stand for?*
YOUNG SCIENTIST: HNO_3? Let me think now... I'm sure I know. It's on the tip of my tongue...
TOP SCIENTIST: *Well, spit it out at once then! It's Nitric Acid!*

Did you know that if you swallowed Uranium you would certainly get atomic ache?

SCIENTIST: *I have just made an incredible discovery: how to make wool out of milk.*
FRIEND: That certainly is extraordinary, but I'm afraid it will make the cow feel a little sheepish!

SCIENCE TEACHER: *Name a liquid that cannot freeze.*
PUPIL: Hot water.

SCIENCE TEACHER: *Light travels at the rate of 186,000 miles per second. Don't you think that's remarkable?*
PUPIL: Not really. It's downhill all the way.

TOP SCIENTIST: *This gas is a deadly poison. What steps would you take if it escaped?*
YOUNG SCIENTIST: Large ones, sir!

Teacher's pet

ANGRY TEACHER: *Why are you so late?*
LAZY PUPIL: Well, I saw the sign in the street that said 'School ahead – go slow!'

ANGRY TEACHER: *I asked you to write a proper essay on the subject of milk, and you have only written two lines when I expected at least two pages. Why?*
PUPIL: I wrote about condensed milk.

TEACHER: *What was the Romans' most remarkable achievement?*
PUPIL: Learning Latin!

HISTORY TEACHER: *Why were the Dark Ages so called?*
PUPIL: Because they had so many knights!

SCIENCE TEACHER: *What is usually used as a conductor of electricity?*
WILLIE: Why, er...
SCIENCE TEACHER: *Wire is correct. Now can you tell me what is the unit of electrical power?*

WILLIE: The what?
SCIENCE TEACHER: *The watt is quite right. Well done, Willie!*

ANGRY PUPIL: *I don't think I deserve nought for this work!*
GRINNING TEACHER: Neither do I, but it's the lowest mark I can give you.

ART TEACHER: *I asked you to draw a pony and trap. You have only drawn the pony.*
ART STUDENT: I thought the pony could draw the trap!

TEACHER: *Willie, what is a cannibal?*
WILLIE: I don't know.
TEACHER: *Well, if you ate your mother and father what would you be then?*
WILLIE: An orphan.

SCIENCE TEACHER: *What is an atom?*
PUPIL: The man who lived in the Garden of Eden with Eve.

TEACHER: *Now, Sally, tell me how many fingers you have.*
SALLY: Ten.
TEACHER: *If you lost four of them in an accident, what would you have then?*
SALLY: No more piano lessons!

JACK: *What is your favourite subject at school?*
JILL: Gozinta.
JACK: *Is that some kind of new language?*
JILL: No, it's just gozinta. You know, two gozinta four, four gozinta eight, eight gozinta sixteen...

TEACHER: *Can anyone in the class use 'fascinate' in a sentence?*

LITTLE WILLIE: I can, Miss.

TEACHER: *All right, Willie. Go ahead.*

LITTLE WILLIE: My duffel coat has ten buttons, but I can only fasten eight.

Under doctor's orders

Why do doctors and nurses wear masks?
So that if someone makes a mistake, no one will know who did it!

DOCTOR: *Are you still taking the cough medicine I gave you?*

PATIENT: No. I tasted it once and decided that I'd rather have the cough.

Once upon a time there was a country doctor who had to visit a patient in a small village. When he arrived at the patient's house, he was interested to see a deep well in the garden. He walked over to the well, but unfortunately tripped just as he reached it, fell into the well and was killed. The moral of this story is simple: Doctors should tend the sick and leave the well alone!

DOCTOR: *Have your eyes ever been checked?*
PATIENT: No, they've always been blue.

PATIENT: *Doctor, will I be able to read when I get my new glasses?*
DOCTOR: You certainly will.
PATIENT: *Oh, that's marvellous. I never knew how to before.*

When is an operation funny?
When it leaves the patient in stitches.

DOCTOR: *What's your average weight?*
PATIENT: I have no idea.
DOCTOR: *Well, what do you think is the most you have ever weighed?*
PATIENT: I'd say about eleven stone.
DOCTOR: *Good. And what do you think is the least you have ever weighed?*
PATIENT: Six pounds, thirteen ounces.

What is the difference between a hill and a pill?
A hill is hard to get up. A pill is hard to get down.

PATIENT: *This ointment makes my arm smart.*
DOCTOR: Why don't you try rubbing some on your head then?

Vituperation

Vituperation means something insulting – and you won't find many insults more insulting than these!

MRS SMITH: *Whenever I'm down in the dumps I get*

myself a new hat.
MRS BROWN: Oh, so that's where you find them!

TOM: *People call you the wonder boy.*
DICK: Do they really?
TOM: *Yes, they just look at you and wonder.*

ROMEO: *You dance very well.*
JULIET: I wish I could say the same for you.
ROMEO: *You could if you were as big a liar as I am.*

JACK: *I throw myself into everything I undertake.*
JILL: Why don't you go and dig a very deep well?

JACK: *Our dog is just like one of the family.*
JILL: Really? Which one?

JACK: *I've changed my mind.*
JILL: I'm so pleased to hear it. Does the new one work any better?

JACK: *Do you feel just like a cup of tea?*
JILL: Oh, yes.
JACK: *I thought so. You look sloppy, wet and hot!*

MRS SMITH: *I'd love you to stay for the night, but I'm afraid you will have to make your own bed.*
MRS BROWN: Oh, I don't mind at all.
MRS SMITH: *Good. Here's a hammer, a saw, and some nails. You'll find the wood in the garage.*

ROMEO: *You remind me of the deep blue sea.*
JULIET: You mean I'm so romantic?
ROMEO: *No, you just make me feel sick.*

Dear Aunt Gussie,

I didn't really forget your birthday. In fact, I was going to send you a present. I had planned to buy you some new handkerchiefs, but I forgot the size of your nose.

Waiter! waiter!

CUSTOMER: *Waiter, this soup is poisonous.*
WAITER: Who told you?
CUSTOMER: *A little swallow.*

WAITER: *Would you like to try some idiot soup, sir?*
CUSTOMER: What's idiot soup?
WAITER: *Thick soup.*

WAITER: *I have frogs' legs, sir.*
CUSTOMER: Don't tell me your troubles. Just bring me a bowl of soup.

CUSTOMER: *I can't eat this revolting food. Call the manager.*
WAITER: It's no use, sir. He can't eat it either.

WAITER: *We have practically everything on the menu, sir.*
CUSTOMER: So I see. Would you bring me a clean one, please?

This section has been censored!

Yarns

Yarns aren't jokes about balls of wool. They are jokes that are a little longer than the average.

Once upon a time a gorilla walked into a coffee bar and ordered a cup of coffee. The man behind the counter was utterly amazed to see a gorilla walk in and to hear one speak, but he brought the coffee right away.

The gorilla drank his coffee in silence and then handed the man a five pound note. The man didn't believe for a moment that the gorilla would know anything about money, so he only gave the gorilla back one pound in change.

'I hope you enjoyed the coffee,' the man said to the gorilla. 'We don't get many gorillas coming in here, you know.'

'At four pounds a cup of coffee,' said the gorilla, 'I'm not surprised.'

Once upon a time there was a lion who wanted to find out why the other animals in the jungle weren't as handsome and strong as he was.

First he asked a zebra. The zebra didn't know. Next he asked a hippopotamus. The hippopotamus didn't know. Next he asked a giraffe. The giraffe didn't know. Next he asked a crocodile. The crocodile didn't know. Next he asked a rhinoceros. The rhinoceros didn't know. Finally the lion came across a little mouse. He looked down at the mouse and said, 'Tell me, mouse, why aren't you as handsome and as strong and as big and as beautiful as I am?'

The little mouse looked up at the lion and said, 'Well, I've not been very well lately.'

Once upon a time there was a pilot who had his own old-fashioned aeroplane. It had an open cockpit and the pilot would sit in the front and his passengers just behind him. One day he offered to take an elderly couple up in the aeroplane. They had never been in a plane before and were very excited.

'You will enjoy the flight,' said the pilot. 'But you must promise to be good and not do any backseat driving.'

The old couple got into the plane and sat behind the pilot. The pilot flew the plane up into the sky and flew around for about twenty minutes. When he landed he said to the old man, 'You did very well for your first flight. I didn't hear a word out of you.'

'That's right,' said the old man. 'It wasn't easy. I almost said something back there when my wife fell out.'

Once upon a time there were three Red Indian squaws. One of them sat outside her wigwam on a leopard skin. Another sat outside her wigwam on a doe skin. The third sat outside her wigwam on a hippopotamus skin. The squaw who was sitting on the leopard skin had just one son. The squaw on the doe skin had just one son too. But the third squaw, the one sitting on the hippopotamus skin, had twin boys. This all goes to prove that the squaw on the hippopotamus is equal to the sons of the squaws on the other two hides!

Once upon a time one of King Arthur's knights came rushing into an inn. There was a terrible storm raging. 'Can you lend me a horse?' the knight asked the innkeeper. 'I have lost my own horse but I must get back to the Court of King Arthur tonight.'

'Oh, Sir Knight,' said the innkeeper, 'alas I have no horse to lend you. The only animal I have is that big, old sheepdog in the corner there.'

'Splendid,' said the knight. 'I shall ride him.'

'Oh no, sir,' said the innkeeper, 'I wouldn't send a knight out on a dog like this!'

Zizz iz ze end

'Zizz is ze end' is what a Frenchman says when you tell him a terrible joke. Well, since this is the end of this unique collection of terrible jokes, here's a final thought to cheer you up if you're feeling sad that you've reached the end of this book.

Don't worry if your job is small
And your rewards are few.
Remember that the mighty oak
Was once a nut like you!

Zat waz ze end of ze Joke Dictionary. Ze Big Book of Practical Jokes beginz over ze page. (The spelling improves there too.)

The BIG Book of PRACTICAL JOKES

INTRODUCTION*

***Specially printed in invisible ink**

Guide to playing practical jokes

Practical jokes are fun to play, but they must be fun for everyone involved. For example, here are TEN practical jokes that must be avoided:

1. Any joke that might hurt a person or animal.
2. Any joke that makes a mess on carpets or furniture.
3. Any joke that makes somebody cry.
4. Any joke that makes anybody cross.
5. Any joke that spoils someone's birthday.
6. Any joke that causes loss of life or limb.
7. Any joke that could give someone a heart attack.
8. Any joke that leaves you homeless.
9. Any joke that results in a world war.
10. Any joke that isn't funny.

Most of the practical jokes in this book can be played on anyone at any time, but always choose your victims very carefully and only ever play practical jokes on someone who will enjoy having the joke played on them. Never play jokes on anyone who is old, frail, nervous, shy or wearing their best clothes.

Have fun!

Gyles

Since this is a book of *crazy* practical jokes we thought we would have the end here. You will find the beginning on the next page – of course.

Post it!

The next time you go out to post a letter, why not play a practical joke or two? So many practical jokes can be played with pillar-boxes.

When you post your letter push your hand inside and grip the edge of the slot so that it looks as if you have got your hand firmly stuck in the box. Don't push your hand in too far, otherwise you might really get stuck! Sooner or later somebody will come along and see you with your hand apparently stuck in the box. Ask them if they will pull your hand out for you. They won't be able to because you will be gripping the inside of the box and however hard they pull your wrist you will appear to be stuck fast.

When the person goes off to get help you can slip your hand out and run! Or you can let the person pull and pull and then suddenly let go and make them think that they have been really strong!

Who's inside?

Another good joke that involves a letter-box is to pretend that somebody is actually *inside* the box! As soon as you see someone coming towards you, start to speak through the slot where you push the letters. Say things like: *'Don't worry, we'll get you out... Are you warm enough in there? Can you breathe all right?'*

Put your ear to the slot to listen for a reply, and peer into the box occasionally as if you could actually see someone. As soon as someone approaches you, look very concerned and tell them that your friend, or the postman, is trapped inside the box and is very frightened. Say that you are just going to get help and ask them to keep talking to the person through the slot just to reassure them that everything will be OK.

Without fail you will find that the victim begins talking to the letter-box, believing that somebody is inside. You run off as if to get help, but actually you run off and hide where you can see the box! You may find the poor victim passing sweets through the slot, or even notes, before they realise that it is all a joke!

Morning mail

Each time you get a letter try to open the envelope very carefully so that you can re-seal it. Collect as many old envelopes as you can, especially ones that have been sent to members of your family, but only keep them if you think that they really look like unopened letters. If you want to be really clever, type out lots of letters and seal them inside the envelopes.

When you have a huge pile, sneak downstairs one night when everyone is in bed and heap the letters on to the doormat so that it looks as if a great stack of mail has arrived. When your mother or father comes downstairs next morning they will hardly believe their eyes when they see the amount of mail they have received. The first few letters on top may even be genuine ones too, that the postman has just delivered, so that it will be even more realistic.

It will not be until they start to open all the letters that they will realise they have been tricked!

Flying snake

You can cause a great laugh when your poor victim opens up a jar or tin and a giant snake comes flying out across the room! This can be especially fun at the tea-table, when your unsuspecting father opens up a jam pot and a metre-long snake leaps out at him!

For this joke you need a very long spring. It must be the kind of spring that will compress right down and when released will spring out to its full length. You can buy these in hardware shops, but it is much easier to make your own, and then you can make it as long as you want.

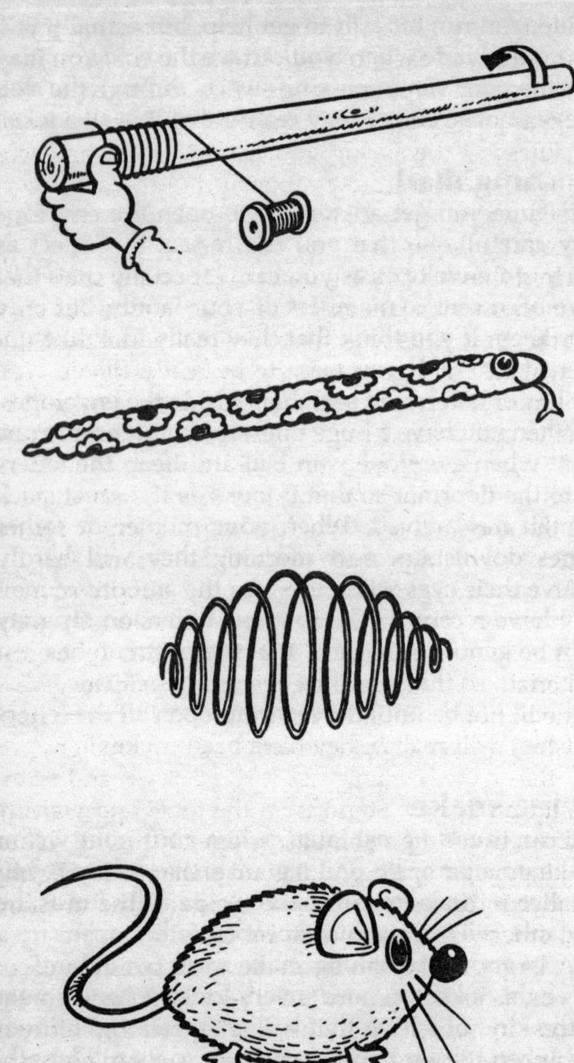

First you will need some wire – something that is quite stiff, but easy to bend, similar to the wire from which paper clips are made. Take a length of rod, such as a garden cane, make sure it is the same thickness as the spring you wish to make, and coil the wire around it. Use a pencil if you want a very small spring, or a walking stick if you want something larger.

Hold the end of the wire in place on the stick with your thumb, and to make the spring *turn the stick*, not the wire. This way you will get a perfect coil. Do not make the coil too tight but allow a few centimetres between each turn. This way you will be able to compress the spring so that it is quite small, and when you release it, it will bounce back to its original shape and size. When you have managed to get the spring the length you want it, slip it off the stick or rod and you are ready to have some fun!

To turn your spring into a snake, simply cover it with a tube of material that is the same length as the fully extended spring. Use a nice green or yellow material, and to make it look more realistic, give it some button eyes and a felt tongue. When you have finished the snake, take an empty, clean mustard pot. Put the snake inside, press it right down and screw the lid on tightly. Stand it on the table and wait for the reaction when somebody opens the lid! When making your spring, make sure that it is slightly smaller in diameter than the inside of the mustard pot, otherwise it will not fit inside.

A larger snake can be made to fit inside a cocoa tin, or a biscuit tin, in fact there is no end to the places in which a flying snake can be hidden. Compressed down into a tiny box you can give it to someone as a Christmas or birthday present. That would certainly be a surprise!

A spring can also be made into a number of other

creatures if you simply use your imagination. A short spring can be turned into a rat or a mouse. All you need to do is make the spring in such a way that the first few coils are smaller than the rest. Then cover the rat with furry material. Give it legs, eyes, nose and a tail, and it is ready for use. Do not, however, try this out on anyone who is frightened of rats, otherwise you could really scare them.

Nail through finger

Ugh! Can you imagine going to your teacher with a nail sticking right through your finger? He or she will probably faint on the spot! So if you want to get out of your maths lesson, this is what to do...

You take a real nail, but don't stick it through your finger, of course! You then ask an adult to bend it for you. Get an adult to do it because they will have the right tools, and you might hurt yourself if you try. The nail should be bent like this:

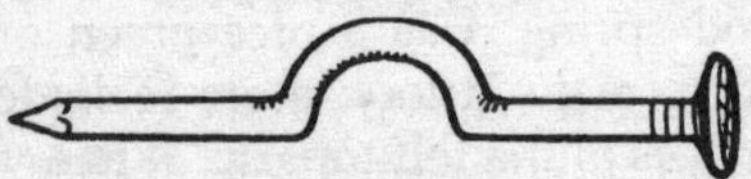

If you slip it over your finger it will look just as if it is going all the way through. For added realism, put a little tomato sauce on your finger, or wrap a bandage round with the nail sticking out. A lot of fun can be had with this.

Finger in matchbox

This is a rather gruesome trick that should not be played upon anyone who might be rather squeamish or nervous. You tell a friend that you have collected something very unusual – you have a real finger in a matchbox. They will not believe you, of course. You then produce a matchbox, slide it open, and inside is a real finger!

To do this trick you don't have to chop off somebody's finger! All you need is a matchbox with a hole in the bottom. In the drawer part of the box you cut a hole just large enough for you to poke your own finger through. If you put a little bit of cotton wool around your finger it will look much more realistic and nobody will see that it is poking through a hole. You then take the other part of the matchbox and on the underside cut a slot. You will then be able to slip the cover over the drawer of the matchbox so that it resembles an ordinary closed box, but when you slowly push the lid open, inside is a...ugh!

Finally, for added realism, draw a line around your finger with a red felt-tip pen so that it really looks as if it has been severed from a hand. You can keep the matchbox in your pocket, and all you have to do is reach inside and quickly poke your finger through the hole before you bring it out. If you hold the box in the correct manner, nobody will realise that it is your finger inside. Last of all, you tell them that the finger is still alive, even though it has been chopped off – and as if by magic the finger starts to wiggle about!

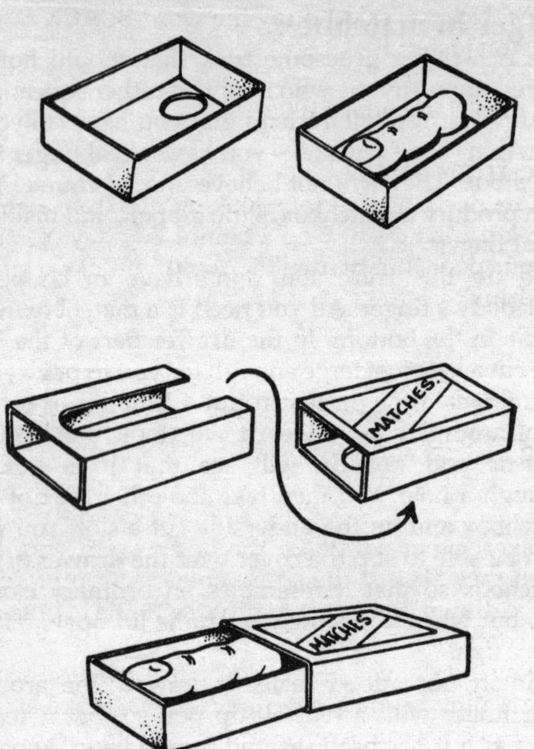

Black and blue

Try this on one of your friends:

You: I bet you I can make you say the word BLACK.
Victim: I bet you can't.
You: I bet you £100 I can.
Victim: OK, try me.
You: What are the colours of the Union Jack?
Victim: Red, white and blue.
You: There! I told you I'd make you say BLUE!

Victim: No, you said I'd say the word BLACK.
You: You just did!

You then claim your £100!

The final straw

You are drinking delicious-looking pop from a bottle with a drinking straw on a boiling hot day. You say to your poor thirsty friend: 'Would you like a sip of my drink?'

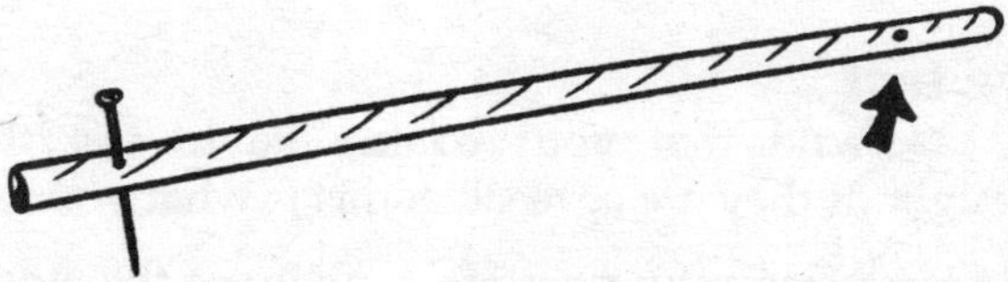

Eagerly they will take the bottle from you, but when they suck at the straw not one drop of drink can be drawn up it. They return the bottle to you and you continue drinking!

How is it done? The secret is in the drinking straw. With a pin you make two holes at each end of the straw, each about five centimetres from the end. If anyone attempts to drink using the straw they will only be able to suck up air, however hard they try. To drink yourself, you only have to cover the two holes at the top with your fingers.

Here is the news

A good trick to play on one of your parents or grandparents is to take their newspaper before they have had a chance to look at it. Remove the outside pages and put them round the centre pages of an old newspaper! When the unsuspecting reader picks up the paper they will read the headlines first and then proceed to the rest of the news. The chances are that they might not notice for a long time that the inside news is a week old!

Another good joke is to glue all the inside pages of an old newspaper together and then swap these old pages for the new inside pages of today's paper. Whoever picks up the paper to read it will not understand why it will not open! You can try this with a friend's comic, or a magazine, but NEVER glue together the pages of a paper or magazine that the owner hasn't read or you could end up in serious trouble!

Eye test

Tell a friend that you would like to test their eyesight. If they are agreeable, this is what you say:

You: First, begin by pointing a finger at the side of your head at eye level.

When their finger is pointing to the side of their head you then say:

You: Now tell me what you can see on my eye chart. There are four letters and a drawing. I'd like you to read out the four letters and tell me what the drawing is.

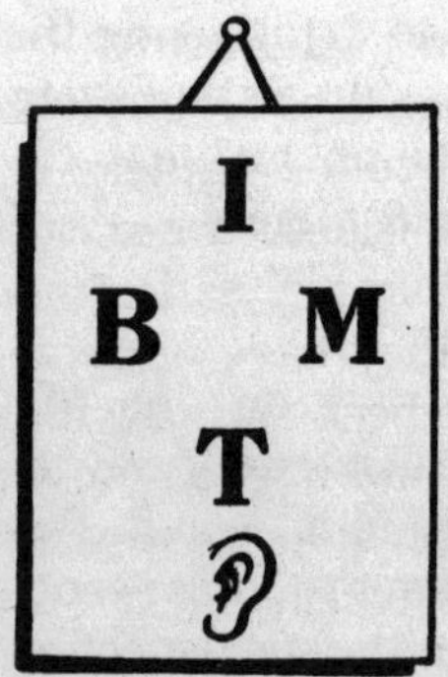

Victim: I, B, M, T, ear.

You: Well, you said it!

What was that?

People always enjoy hearing about ghosts and I think everyone secretly hopes that one day they will see or hear something spooky, but how would they really react if they suddenly heard ghostly moans in the night or the clanking of chains?

If you have a tape recorder, you can find out. Take a tape that is 120 minutes long, that is, an hour on each side. On one side, wind the tape on to approximately halfway so that the first half an hour is blank. On the remainder of the tape, record a few ghostly noises. Moan and wail gently like a demented spirit. Rattle a piece of chain so that it makes an eerie clanking sound; record some ghostly footsteps, or an ear-piercing scream – anything that sounds out of this world.

Once you have made this tape you can use it in a number of ways. Just before your friends arrive, hide the tape recorder somewhere in the room and switch it on. Remember that the first half an hour is blank, so there will be no sound. When your friends have arrived and settled down, turn the conversation to ghosts. You could even say that your own house is supposed to be haunted, and start to tell your friends about the ghost who is said to roam the house – perhaps a grey lady who seems to be searching for something, or a headless knight who clanks around, even a shapeless hooded figure.

Just when your friends are starting to feel a little scared, without warning, eerie, ghostly sounds will start. Obviously they have nothing to do with you because you have been sitting with your friends for the last half hour and haven't moved! If you appear to be scared too it will look even more realistic.

Another way in which you can use your tape is to put it on and hide it just before you are going out and the rest of the family are left alone in the house. You can be miles away in the half an hour before the noises start. End the tape by saying: 'This is a practical joke . . . this is a practical joke . . .'

Down the drain

For this practical joke you will need an old door key that nobody wants any more. Make quite certain that it is of absolutely no use to anyone before you take it. Most people have a few old keys lying around somewhere, so have a look in your garage or garden shed, or at the backs of drawers.

Having got the key, make sure it looks clean, and make a key ring for it from a curtain ring, so that it looks like your door key. Tell your friends that your mother is out and has let you have the key to the door so that you can let yourself in.

As you walk along, throw it into the air casually a few times and catch it. Then, to your friends' amazement, throw it in the air and instead of catching it, let it fall down a drain. Their faces will be a picture because they will think that this really is your door key. After they have tried unsuccessfully to fish it out for you, you can let on that it is all a joke. Then run home as fast as you can!

Say 'Cheese'

To get your family really worried, all you need is an ordinary camera with *no film in it*. Then, when people are least suspecting it, you start snapping pictures of them in embarrassing situations.

Pretend to take a picture of grandma coming out of the bathroom without her teeth, or your mother with cold cream all over her face and curlers in her hair, your brother just getting out of the bath, or your sister sunbathing in the garden. You then say that you promise not to have the film developed if they give you a sweet, or 50p! You then reveal that the camera was empty all the time!

Dotty problem

Give your friend a pencil and a piece of paper. Tell them that you will give them 50p if they can write a small letter 'I' with a dot over it.

Naturally they will think it is very easy and will write:

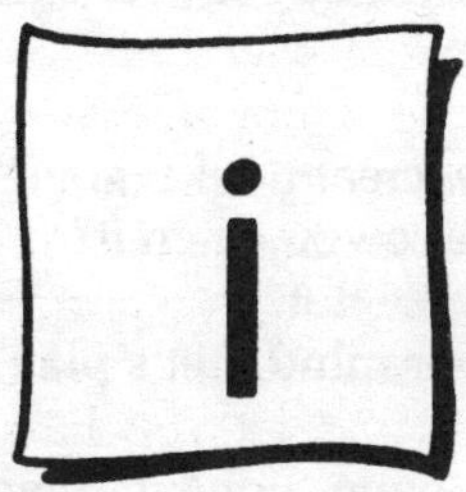

You then shout 'wrong!' and show that a small letter 'I' with a dot over it really looks like the drawing below:

Now collect your 50p!

Wakey-wakey

This is an *alarming* trick to play on your brother or sister (providing they do not sleep in the same room as yourself), or anyone else in the household who is a very heavy sleeper and has difficulty waking up in the morning.

Gather together as many alarm clocks as you can,

at least five or six, and set them to go off at five-minute intervals. One might go off at eight o'clock, the next at five past, the next at ten-past eight, and so on. Or if you wish you can set them so that they all go off at exactly the same time. Your unfortunate victim will not know what has hit him or her, and if that doesn't get them out of bed then nothing will!

Greedy pig

You: Where's my cream cake gone? It was here a minute ago. Have you eaten it?
Victim: No, of course not.
You: Oh well, never mind. Let's play a game.
Victim: OK.
You: I'll start by saying 'I one it', then you say 'I two it', and I'll say 'I three it', and so on.
Victim: OK.
You: I one it.
Victim: I two it.
You: I three it.
Victim: I four it.
You: I five it.
Victim: I six it.
You: I seven it.
Victim: I eight it.
You: There! I knew you had, you greedy pig!

Monster fun

Next time it snows you can play this joke and fool people into believing that some incredible monster has walked across your garden. Maybe it was the famous yeti, or the well-known 'big foot'.

All you need are a couple of buckets and a stick. Put the buckets on your feet, and by holding on to the handles you will find that you are able to walk quite easily. As you take giant strides through the snow you will leave giant marks. If you stop after each couple of steps and draw some marks of toes or claws in the snow with your stick you can make each footprint look quite realistic.

When you have left quite a trail, hide the buckets and say nothing. If you start shouting that you have seen the abominable snowman people might be a little suspicious, but if you say absolutely nothing and let *somebody* else discover the prints you will find that it is much more fun.

Don't ever let on that it really was you, and you can keep everyone guessing for a long time to come!

Holy! Holy! Holy!

Get an adult to punch a large hole in the middle of an old teaspoon for you. A plastic teaspoon will do. Now place the spoon in a sugar basin and wait for someone to try and spoon some sugar into their tea. They will find it impossible!

It's started!

Does your mother have a favourite television programme? Lots of people have a favourite drama or soap opera that they like to watch, whether it is *EastEnders* or *Coronation Street*. If your mother has a favourite programme that she rarely misses, see if you can make a tape-recording of the theme music to this programme. The theme music of quite a number of top television programmes is available on a tape, too, if you can afford it.

Five minutes before the programme is due to start, your mother is sure to nip out to make a cup of tea, or pay a quick visit to the bathroom. Immediately you put on your tape-recording so that the familiar theme music comes floating through the air.

You shout: 'Mum! It's started!' She will come charging into the room believing that the programme has begun and thinking that she is missing something. You can then shout: 'Fooled you!'

If you are lucky, the programme really will start within a short time, so there will not be long enough for you to be told off!

Housey-housey

You: I bet you I can jump higher than a house.
Victim: I bet you can't.
You: I bet you £1.00 that I can.
Victim: I bet you £1.00 you can't.
You: I'll have my £1.00 now please. A HOUSE CAN'T JUMP!

Ring dem bells!

If you have a small tape recorder you will already have seen that you can have lots of fun with it, playing tricks on people. Apart from recording noises and music, you can record everyday sounds and put them to good use.

One such sound is that of a telephone ringing. Leave your tape recorder beside the telephone and the next time it rings, switch the recorder on and tape the telephone bell. Don't allow the phone to ring for too long or the caller might ring off! If you want a longer ring, then get your friend to ring you up at a specific time and you can record the ringing for as long as you wish, as you will know that you don't have to answer it.

Now that you have got the sound on tape, you can make the telephone ring whenever you want. Imagine the surprise when the person coming to answer it finds that it stops ringing just before they pick it up. Or if you want to be a real horror, make the phone ring when your father is in the bath!

Aaaaaaaaggghhhh!

Walk into your classroom at school, point to the floor and go: 'Aaaaaaggghhh! Look at that huge spider on the floor over there! Aaaaaaaagggggghhhhhhh!!'

Immediately everyone will leap up on to their desks yelling: 'Where?'

'Help!'

'Shrieeeeeeeeeeeeeeeeeek!!'

After a couple of minutes you shout: 'April fool!'

Whoops!

The next time somebody breaks a piece of china, see if you can VERY VERY CAREFULLY save some of the larger pieces without cutting yourself. Often broken china isn't sharp at all, but it might be safest to wear gloves when you pick up the pieces.

Put the bits inside a box with a lid (a small shoe box would do) and seal the box carefully with tape so that no pieces fall out. The loose crockery inside will now rattle about freely.

Cover the box with a sheet of pretty wrapping paper so that it looks like a beautiful present. The next time somebody has a birthday, walk into the room carrying this box. As you walk towards them you let the box accidentally (on purpose) slip through your fingers. SMASH! WHOOPS!

Looking dismayed, you say how sorry you are but

you seem to have broken the present. After a few minutes you smile, and produce the *real* present.

This joke can be used over and over again providing the box is sealed very, very tightly, because it doesn't matter how many pieces the crockery inside breaks into. If you do not have any pieces of broken crockery to put in the box, you might find that somebody has an old, chipped cup and saucer they do not want, or you might pick one up at a jumble sale for just a few pence. Do not break the cup and saucer, but simply place them both in the box and seal the box up tightly. When you drop the 'present' you will get the smashing noise you require.

To make the joke even more effective, try and let the box fall to the floor just as the person is about to take it from you so that it looks as if it is their fault! Whoops, butter-fingers!

Things that go bump in the night

With the help of a piece of cotton and a small stick you can produce a spooky creature that goes tap, tap, tap, on somebody's window in the middle of the night – even if you live in a tall block of flats!

Once the curtains are drawn across, tie a small stick on to a length of cotton, tie the cotton to the window stay on the inside, and hang the stick outside the window.

It helps if it is a windy night. Sooner or later the wind will cause the stick to tap against the window when your victim is in bed trying to get to sleep. They will be too frightened to draw the curtains back to have a look for fear of the creature that might be outside!

Things that go pop in the night

With the aid of some dried peas, an empty yogurt pot or cream carton, and a tin tray, you can create the most amazing practical joke.

In your victim's bedroom hide the metal tray on which you have stood the pot full of dried peas. On top of the wardrobe is a good place, or under a dressing table, but make sure it is somewhere that the victim will not see it.

Just before he or she goes to bed, pour some hot water on to the peas. The water will soak into the peas, causing them to expand and pop out of the carton, landing on the tray and making quite a noise. Your poor victim will not be able to work out what the noise is!

Experiment in the privacy of your own room first so that you can see how it works. An upside-down biscuit tin makes an excellent noise when the peas land on it, too, and the higher up the yogurt carton is from the tin, the louder the sound will be. Try it and see what happens!

What am I?

You: Ask me if I am a boat.
Victim: Are you a boat?
You: Yes, I am. Now ask me if I am a train.
Victim: Are you a train?
You: No, I've just told you I'm a boat!

Look up

This is a very old practical joke, but it never fails to work, even though people have been playing this trick for hundreds and thousands of years.

The next time you are out in a busy street with some friends, suddenly stop and look up at the sky. Point at it. Tap your friend on the shoulder and point so that he looks up too.

Before you know where you are, everybody that passes by will be looking up at the sky too. It always works. Try it!

How far?

The next time somebody is leaving your house and you have said 'goodbye' to them at the door, let them get just a little way down the road and then call them back. You beckon them to the door and then you lean towards them confidentially and say: 'How far would you have got if I hadn't called you back?'

You can catch people out every time, and it never fails to raise a laugh.

Make a monkey

Put ten matches on the table and ask your friend to make the word monkey out of them. He will try but is sure to fail. You then show him how it is done.

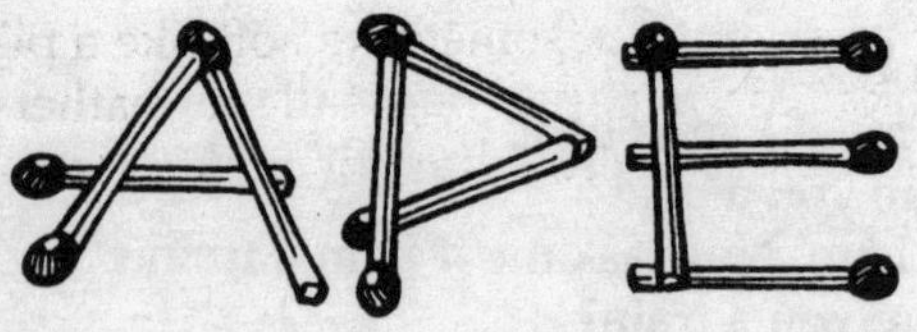

Well, an ape is very like a monkey, isn't it?

Dribbler!

Take an ordinary paper cup, and with a pin make a few small holes just below the rim so that they cannot be seen. Now fill the cup with water, or lemonade, and give it to a friend to drink. Pour yourself some in an ordinary paper cup so that your friend does not suspect that anything suspicious is going on.

When your friend tries to drink from the cup, the liquid will dribble through the holes all over him. However he tries to drink, he won't be able to do it without some of the drink dribbling down his chin. You, of course, drink away quite happily, whilst he will be unable to work out why he keeps getting in a mess. Only you will know the secret!

Go on ahead

This is one of the oldest practical jokes in the whole world! You balance something on top of a door that is slightly ajar so that when your victim walks into the room and pushes the door open, whatever is on top of the door will fall on their head, and you fall about laughing.

You must be very, very careful indeed when you do this joke. NEVER PUT ANYTHING HEAVY ON TOP OF THE DOOR. This could be extremely dangerous. Don't go putting buckets of water on top of doors either, or anything that will spill and make a horrible mess, but put something soft like a pillow or a cushion, or a paper bag full of feathers or confetti, so that it doesn't hurt or make a mess of your victim.

Too much!

Catch your friends out with this:

You: What does T O spell?

Victim: To.
You: And what does T O O spell?
Victim: Too.
You: What does T W O spell?
Victim: Two.
You: And what is the second day of the week?
Victim: Tuesday.
You: Wrong! Monday is the second day of the week.

Touch the ground

The next time you see somebody riding past on a bicycle, point to the back wheel of the bicycle and shout: 'Your back wheel's touching the ground!'

Almost certainly your victim will get off his bike and stop to have a look at his back wheel! It also works if you shout: 'Your front wheel's going round!'

It's a very old trick, but it still works!

How many fingers?

Tell your friend that you have *eleven* fingers. They won't believe you, so you prove that you have. Count from one to ten on your fingers, then count backwards – 10, 9, 8, 7, 6 – plus five fingers on your other hand makes eleven!

Barking at the moon

You: What has six legs and barks at the moon?
Victim: I don't know. What?
You: A dog.
Victim: A dog?
You: Yes, I added on two extra legs to make it harder.

Water! Water!

Take a large hat or a box, and a glass of water. Stand the glass of water on a table and cover it with the hat.

Now tell your friends that you can drink the water

from the glass without touching the hat. You then crouch down under the table and make a loud slurping noise, just as if you are drinking water. You stand up and say: 'There, I told you I could drink from the glass without touching the hat.'

Someone is sure to lift the hat to see if the water has disappeared, at which point you grab the glass and drink the water. You have been able to drink from the glass, and you *haven't touched the hat* – which is exactly what you said you would do!

Three wise monkeys

You: There were three wise monkeys sitting on a wall. Their names were Doh, Ray, and Me. Doh and Ray jumped off the wall. Which monkey was left?

Victim: Me.

Take notice

This is one of the most popular practical jokes of all, especially in the classroom.

Take a piece of paper about ten centimetres square, and write a message on it. Write something like I AM VERY STUPID, or something practical like KISS ME QUICK, or TAP ME ON THE SHOULDER.

Fix a little piece of sticky tape on the top of the notice and try and attach it to your victim's back without him realising what you are doing. The easiest way to do this is to pat him gently on the back in a friendly greeting, so that he doesn't notice that you have stuck something on him. He will not realise why people keep laughing all day long!

If you have put a very practical message on his back, such as PAT ME ON THE HEAD, he will wonder why people keep patting him on the head all day long. Another way of putting a message on someone's back, especially if you go to the kind of school where you have to wear a school uniform and have a dark-coloured blazer, is to write a message in chalk on the palm of your hand. When you pat your victim on the back the message will be transferred to his or her blazer. The chalk will brush off quite easily when the victim does realise what has happened. If you are going to do a chalk message in this way, remember to write the message *backwards* on your palm so that when it is pressed on to the victim's back it will appear the right way round, otherwise it will not make any sense.

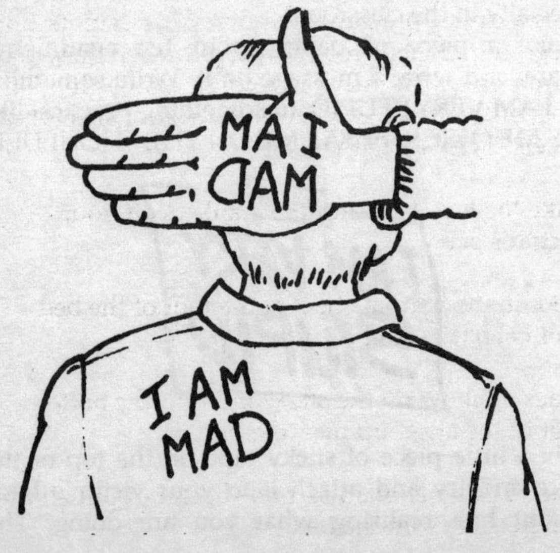

Jumping jacks

Try this on one of your friends:
You: I bet you that I can jump across the street.
Victim: I bet you can't.
You: I bet you £100 I can.
Victim: I bet you £100 you can't.
You: OK then!

You then very carefully cross the road, and when you are standing across the street, you jump!

Ting-a-ling-a-ling!

From a pet shop, buy some tiny bells that are meant to be hung in budgie cages. These are very cheap to buy, costing only a few pence each, so get as many as you can afford.

Tie them to the springs underneath your victim's bed where they cannot be seen. Every time he or she gets in and out of bed, or moves about, a bell will ring!

Apple-pie bed

This is a classic practical joke that your parents, and even grandparents, probably played when they were children. It is still great fun to play, although it isn't so easy if the bed has a duvet instead of sheets and blankets! This is what you do:

1 Take the top sheet and the blankets off your victim's bed.

2 Loosen the bottom sheet at the foot of the bed, and keep it tucked in at the top.

3 Place a pillow on the sheet and fold the bottom half of the sheet up over the pillow.

4 Don't bother about a second sheet, but put all the blankets back on the bed.

5 Finally, fold the untucked end of the sheet back over the top of the blankets and it will *look* like the top end of the sheet that isn't there!

The bed now looks quite normal and nobody will realise that it has even been touched. When your victim goes to bed, however, he or she will discover that it is far from normal, and will only be able to put his or her feet down a few centimetres.

Lumps and bumps

This is fun to do if you are staying at the seaside, especially if you are sharing a bedroom with some friends, or a brother or sister. Gather from the beach a few small round pebbles. When your victim is out of the room, put some of these pebbles under the bottom sheet of his or her bed.

Put them about three-quarters of the way down, not near the top otherwise they will be seen when the victim turns the cover back to get into bed. It will not be until he or she is actually in bed and puts his or her feet towards the bottom that the victim will discover just how lumpy the bed is!

Kicking against the pricks

This bedtime joke needs a nice prickly hairbrush, or preferably two or three if you can muster them. When your victim is out of the room, turn back the bedclothes and array the brushes towards the bottom of the bed, out of sight when the bedclothes are turned back for the victim to climb into bed but not so far down that his or her feet won't come into contact with them. The poor victim will think that he or she has climbed into a nest of hedgehogs!

What a glass!

Take an ordinary drinking glass or tumbler and fill it

approximately three-quarters full of lemonade or cola. Then take a piece of cling film, the kind that sticks to itself and is used to cover food and keep it fresh. Stretch a piece across the top of the glass and smooth it down the sides so that it cannot be seen.

You will find that if you use a very small piece, only slightly larger than the top of the glass, you will be able to stretch it so that it is completely invisible. Now give the glass to your friend to drink! It will look like a very ordinary glass of drink until they put it to their lips, but then they will find that not one drop of the drink comes out, however far back they tilt it.

Try it when you are next allowed to pass guests glasses of wine or sherry, and watch their faces as they elegantly try to take a sip of their wine!

This joke can be played the other way round by placing an invisible film over an empty glass so that when somebody tries to pour something inside it won't go! But this can turn out to be rather messy if you are not careful, so it is best to attempt it only in the kitchen or in the garden.

Ear! Ear!

You: What is high and white and cold and has a summit and ears?
Victim: I don't know, what?
You: A mountain, of course.
Victim: But where are the ears on a mountain?
You: Haven't you heard of mountaineers?

Too tight

If you want to make a member of your family think that their feet have grown overnight, or that their shoes have shrunk, simply stuff a ball of newspaper in the toes of their shoes. When they try to put them on in the morning they will find that their feet will not go in! If you do this to every pair of shoes that they have they will really begin to think that their feet have swollen.

Yes Siam

You: Many years ago in the ancient kingdom of Siam there was a very secret society that only the cleverest and the richest people in the country could belong to.

Victim: Really?

You: Yes, and the society still exists, but now that Siam has changed its name to Thailand the society is more secret than it has ever been. I am a member of the society, of course.

Victim: Oh yes?

You: I'll let you join if you want.

Victim: OK, what do I have to do?

You: Well, it's very simple. Just close your eyes and spin round five times. Then repeat the ancient oath of the kingdom of Siam five times. It's in Siamese:
OOO WATA NA SIAM!

On the telly

Say to a friend at school: 'Did you have your television on last evening?'

When they say 'yes' you ask: 'How did it fit?'

Black mark

Borrow some of your mother's dark eyeshadow. Don't put it around your eyes, but put a little on your finger.

Now tell a friend that she has a black mark on the side of her nose. Tell her to stand still and you will wipe it off. You pretend to wipe away the smudge that isn't there, and actually put one on!

She will then go off, happy that you have wiped

the embarrassing mark from her nose, not realising how funny she looks.

Strong man

Sit cross-legged on the floor.

Now place your right hand on top of your head with your fingers spread out as far as it is possible for them to go.

Now bet anyone absolutely anything you like that they will not be able to take hold of your forearm just above the elbow and lift your hand off your head. However hard they try they won't be able to do it.

What price?

You: The Princess of Wales is going to open a new tellycost near us next week.

Victim: What's a tellycost?

You: Oh, about £150.

Big drip!

This practical joke takes a little preparation.

Find an empty plastic squash bottle with a tightly-fitting plastic top. Take a pin and make about ten tiny holes in the bottom of the bottle. Now hold the bottle over the kitchen sink and fill it right up to the brim with water, and as soon as it is full put the cap on and dry the bottle carefully.

Now select your victim and tell him that you are having terrible trouble getting the top off this bottle of water and could he help you. Give him the bottle.

The moment he takes the cap off the bottle the water will begin to pour through the tiny holes and he will get wet! Don't play this joke on anyone who is wearing his best clothes, and don't give it to anyone who is standing in the middle of the living-room carpet, either!

Ties up!

For this you must have a victim who wears a tie…

You: What does a boat do when it gets into harbour?
Victim: Drops anchor.
You: No.
Victim: Sounds its horn?
You: No.
Victim: Turns off its engines?
You: No.
Victim: What does it do then?
You: Ties up!

You then flick the victim's tie up and over his head as you say: 'TIES UP!'

What a number

This will catch most people out, unless they are really mathematically minded. Don't try it on your teacher!

Give your victim a piece of paper and a pencil and say that they have ten seconds to write down the number eleven thousand, eleven hundred and eleven.

You will find that most people write down:

11,1111

or even:

11,1100,11

However they write it you will invariably find that it is WRONG!

The correct answer is 12,111 (of course!).

A nice how-d'ye-do!

You meet someone in the street whom you haven't

seen for a long time. Naturally you will want to shake hands with him. What he won't realise is that you have a teaspoonful of raspberry jam in the palm of your hand! The look of his face will have to be seen to be believed – in fact it might be a long time before you see him again!

Stick 'em up!

This practical joke will prove to your friends that not only can you fool them, you can also exercise great power over them and make them do things that you want them to do, even if they don't want to do them themselves.

Here's how. Get your victim to stand in a doorway and push the *backs* of her hands against the frame of the door as hard as she possibly can for exactly one minute. It must be for one minute otherwise the trick will not work.

When the time is up ask her to move away from the door, and as she does so shout: 'Stick 'em up!'

Whether she wants to or not her arms will automatically rise into the air! What great power you have!

Finger through hole

This joke will always catch people out. Take an ordinary piece of paper, and put a very small hole in the centre of it. Make sure the hole is too small for anybody's finger to go through.

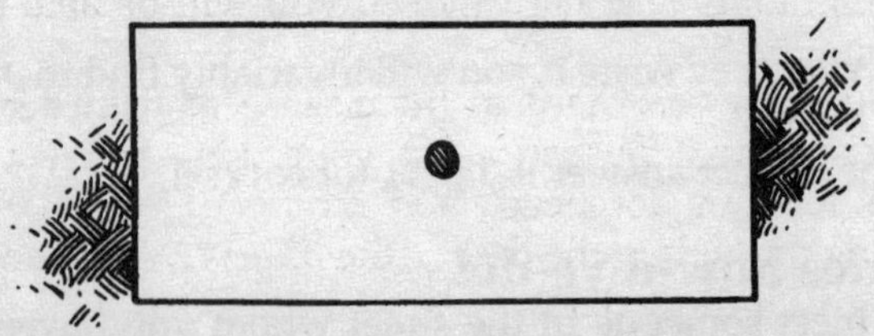

Then challenge someone to push their finger through the centre of the paper without tearing it. Nobody will be able to do it.

When everyone has given up, simply roll the paper up into a tube and push your finger down the centre of the tube!

Finger tips

Stand squarely on both feet, with just the tips of your forefingers touching as in the diagram.

Now you can bet anybody absolutely anything you like that they will not be strong enough to grasp you by the wrists and pull your fingers apart.

If they hold you by the wrists, no matter how strong they are, they won't be able to do it. They really won't!

The date

Ask a friend to take a coin from his pocket and hold it very tightly in his hand. Tell him that by concentrating very hard indeed you will be able to tell him the date.

You stare very hard at his closed hand in deep concentration. You screw up your eyes, put your hand to your forehead, and say: 'Yes, yes... it's coming through... the date... the date is...' and you then give today's date!

What's that smell?

You: If frozen water is iced water, what is frozen ink?
Victim: Iced ink.
You: Oh, I wondered what the smell was!

Answer the question

You: I am going to ask you three questions. To each of the three questions you can either answer 'yes' or 'no' – but you mustn't speak. You can only give me your answer with your fingers.

This is what you do. Make a circle with your thumb and your little finger by pressing the nail of your little finger into the underside of the thumb, like this:

Now hold your other three fingers together and press them down flat on the edge of a table, like this:

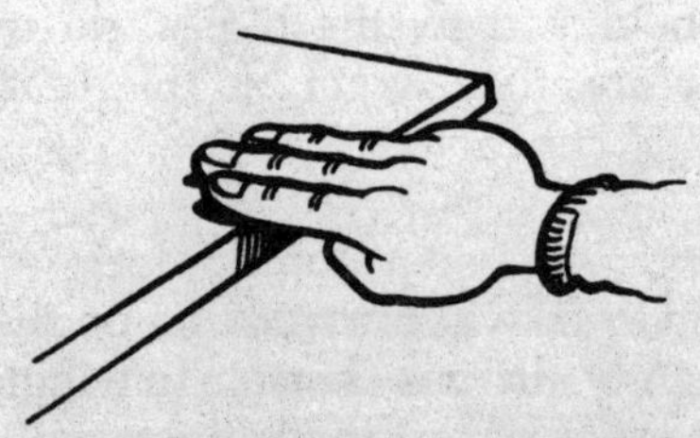

To answer Question One you must use the finger next to your thumb.
To answer Question Two you must use your middle finger.
To answer Question Three you must use your third finger.

If you want to answer 'yes', just wiggle the finger in question. To answer 'no', lift the finger three

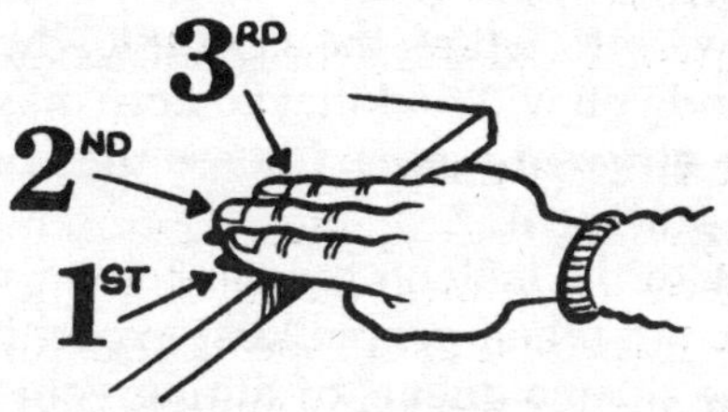

centimetres away from the table. When answering a question you must not move any of your other fingers or your thumb.

I will now ask you three questions.

Question One. Are you feeling happy today?
(Your victim can answer either 'yes' or 'no' by wiggling the first finger or by lifting it three centimetres off the table.)

Question Two. Is your birthday this month?
(The victim can answer either 'yes' or 'no' by wiggling the middle finger or by lifting it three centimetres off the table.)

Question Three. Are you a stupid idiot?
(Your poor victim will find that he or she can only answer 'yes' because it is possible to wiggle the third finger, but virtually impossible to lift it three centimetres off the table without moving the other fingers!)

Naughty balloon

Take an ordinary balloon. Blow some air into it, but do not tie the neck. Instead, let the air out very slowly, pulling the neck as you do so.

You will discover that as the air escapes from the balloon it will make some extremely funny noises! Try it a few times, letting the air out slowly, then very quickly, and you will find that you can make a whole variety of different noises. Choose the one you like best, and practise it.

Now, with the balloon hidden behind your back, let the air out when people least expect it – on the bus, in the cinema queue, or during your final end-of-term lesson – and see the reaction!

The catch

You need to be very rich for this trick because you need a £5 note. Tell your victim that they can *have* the note *if* they can catch it when you drop it.

It sounds an easy way of getting money, but it isn't. Hold the note at one end, and ask him or her to hold a finger and thumb on either side of the note, but not actually touching it.

Tell your victim that you are going to let the note go at any time and he or she must catch it between the thumb and forefinger. Do not drop the note immediately but keep talking for a while, saying: 'I am going to drop the note any moment now, but I'm not going to tell you exactly when I'm going to drop it so you really will have to be very quick...'

Suddenly, in mid-sentence, let the note go. However quick the victim's reflexes are, the note will have slipped down to the floor before he or she has had time to realise that the note has gone.

If you are worried that it just might not work, try it with a piece of paper first. That way you will not lose any money. Only when you are really confident that you can drop it without it being caught can you attempt the trick with a note.

If your victim seems to have really quick reflexes,

then you can simply try the trick with a £1 coin. Let them hold the thumb and forefinger as close to the coin as they like. Because of the weight of the coin they will never be able to catch it, because it will have clanged to the floor before they even have time to think about it.

Loose thread

Mothers have a habit of pulling loose threads and pieces of cotton off people's clothes. If your mother, or a friend's mother, has a habit of doing this then you can play a practical joke on her.

All you need is a reel of cotton in a similar colour to the jacket you are wearing, and a needle. Thread the needle with the cotton without cutting it, and push it through the jacket from the inside to the outside so that just a few centimetres of cotton show.

Remove the needle and put it away safely. Put the rest of the reel of cotton in an inside jacket pocket, and walk around as if everything were normal.

Sooner or later some eagle-eyed person will spot the cotton, and try and remove it for you. As soon as she has the end of the cotton in her hand, walk away

from her as fast as you possibly can. Your astonished victim will be left holding a piece of cotton that gets longer and l o n g e r and l o n g e r !

Keep your eyes open

You: You'd better keep your eyes open tomorrow.
Victim: Why?
You: Otherwise you'll bump into things!

With my ear

Take a piece of paper and a pencil. Say to your victim: 'I can write with my left ear!'

Of course, she will not believe you and is certain to say: 'Go on then!'

You then take the pencil and paper and write

Under water

You: I bet you that I can sing under water.
Victim: I bet you can't!
You: I bet you 50p I can.
Victim: All right! I bet you 50p you can't!

Immediately take a glass full of water and hold it up above your head and start to sing. You are under water, and you are singing, so collect your money!

Singing in the rain

For this practical joke you will need a box of confetti, which you can buy quite cheaply from a newsagent or a stationery shop. If you can't afford to buy confetti, make some yourself by cutting up lots of pieces of coloured tissue paper.

The next time there is a rainy day, go into the library or school cloakroom, wherever there is a row of umbrellas, and put some confetti inside each umbrella. As soon as the victims go outside and open the umbrellas they will be covered in showers of confetti!

Sliced bananas

Imagine the look on your victim's face when he next eats a banana, only to discover when he peels it that it is already sliced.

Once you know how, you can secretly slice bananas and apples when they are still INSIDE THEIR SKINS! Here's what you do.

Take a needle and push it into the banana along the length of one of the seams, like this:

Now wiggle the needle from side to side and it will be cutting the banana inside the skin. Put the needle in at several points up and down the length of the banana and you can slice as many pieces as you want.

When your victim peels his banana, he will be astonished to see it fall to pieces! If you do this to every banana in a bunch, or in a fruit bowl, it will happen whichever banana he picks up. Or if you wish, put two bananas in a fruit bowl, one sliced and one not. If he takes the sliced one then he will be in for a shock, especially as yours is still whole. If by any chance he takes the whole one, then you can bet him 50p that you can magically slice your banana without even peeling it – and you do!

Granny Smith's!

You can slice up an apple in exactly the same way as the bananas which would even shock Granny Smith! This isn't quite so easy though.

For this joke you require a needle and thread. Thread the needle and pass it through the apple from one side to the other, going as close to the apple skin as you can, like this:

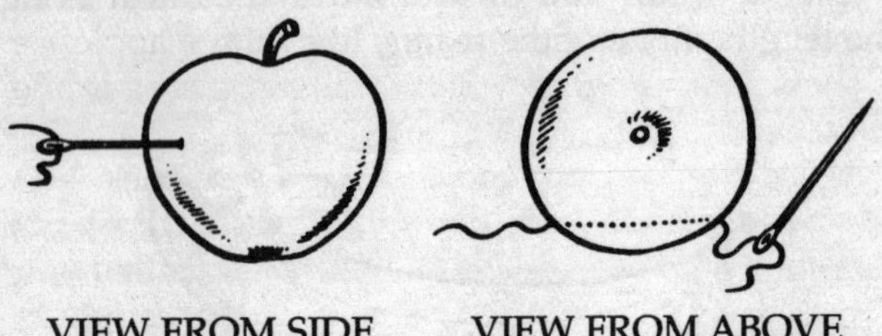

VIEW FROM SIDE VIEW FROM ABOVE

Now push the needle through the apple again, like this:

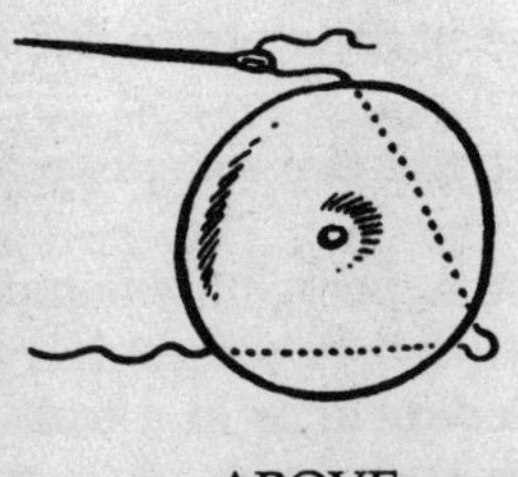

ABOVE

and finally push the needle and thread through the apple for the last time, like this:

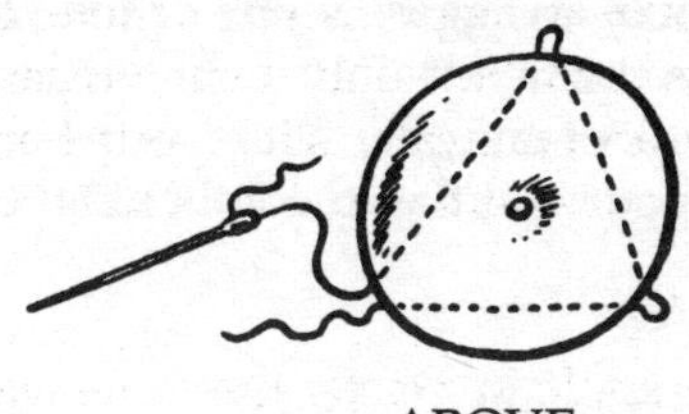

ABOVE

If you carefully tug at the two ends of the thread you will be able to slice through the apple with the thread right through the centre. Do this gently so that you do not tear the apple's skin. All there should be on the outside are three tiny pin holes where the needle has gone through, which nobody will even notice. When your victim starts to peel the apple, he or she will be amazed when it falls in pieces in the hand!

Again, you can pretend to do a magic trick, and wave your hands over the apple causing it to cut itself in pieces. Or you can tell your friends that you are so strong that you can actually *pull* an apple in pieces. No one will believe it, but seeing is believing!

Do you get the yolk?

You: How do you spell the word 'joke'?
Victim: J, O, K, E.
You: How do you spell the word 'folk'?
Victim: F, O, L, K.
You: How do you spell the word 'poke'?
Victim: P, O, K, E.
You: How do you spell the white of an egg?
Victim: Y, O, L, K.
You: That's the yellow of an egg!
The white of an egg is albumen – A, L, B, U, M, E, N.

Another egg yolk joke that is bound to catch people out is to ask which of the following two statements is correct – the yolk of an egg *are* white or the yolk of an egg *is* white? Almost certainly your victim will tell you that 'the yolk of an egg *is* white' is the correct answer. You then point out that the yolk of an egg is YELLOW!

Unmeltable!

Find some clear plastic in the shops. This can usually be found in hardware stores or Do-It-Yourself shops. Ask an adult to cut the plastic up into small cubes for you so that they look just like ice-cubes.

These can be used in many ways. You can put them in an ice-tray and store them in the freezer compartment of your fridge. The next time some unsuspecting person wants to cool their drink down they will put these lumps of plastic in their glass! Alternatively, you can invite your friends round one summer's day and offer them a glass of lemonade. Put some of your joke ice-cubes in their glasses and watch their faces as they wonder why the ice doesn't melt!

Frothing sugar

If someone in your family takes too much sugar in their tea, you can soon put a stop to it by giving them frothing sugar. What you need is a large jar of liver salts, which can be bought at any chemist or supermarket.

Take an empty sugar basin and fill it with this white powder. Unless your victim looks very closely, he will not notice that it isn't sugar. When he takes a spoonful, however, he will quickly notice the difference. Immediately a spoonful of this sugar is put into tea, something quite astonishing will happen. The tea will start to bubble and froth, and will overflow into the saucer. This will probably put your victim off sugar for life!

Floating sugar

If you use sugar lumps instead of granulated sugar, you can still play a joke on your sugar-taking friends. Find some pieces of white polystyrene foam. These are often used as protective packing, or they can be bought for only a few pence from hardware shops.

Cut the polystyrene into cubes so that it resembles sugar cubes, and place them in a sugar basin. If your victim puts them into his tea with a spoon or with some sugar tongs he will probably not even notice that it isn't real sugar – that is, until he sees the lumps *floating* on top of his tea!

The first and last time

Tell your victim that you are going to show him something that has never been seen before by human eyes, and will never be seen again. This will really mystify him.

You then take a peanut shell and open it up, taking out the peanut (this peanut has never been seen before by anyone!) and you pop it in your mouth and swallow it (so it will never ever be seen again by anyone!) and you have shown him exactly what you said you would!

Muddle head!

You: I want you to add these things up.
Victim: OK. What?
You: One ton of sawdust
One ton of chewing gum
One ton of fat
One ton of nothing
One ton of bone

Have you got all that in your head?
Victim: Yes.
You: I thought so!

Money walks

You need two things for this practical joke. The first is you have to be rich, because you need a £5 note, and the second is that you will need to have very quick reactions – otherwise you could end up £5 poorer!

With a piece of adhesive tape, stick a length of cotton on to the note. Lay the note down on the pavement and hide behind a fence or tree, hanging on firmly to the thread. Soon somebody will come along and bend down to pick up the note. As soon as they bend down you must whisk the note away as quickly as you possibly can.

Toffee pommes

Do you enjoy toffee-apples? You can buy them at the seaside and at fairgrounds, but it is just as easy to make them at home. Ask your mother to make you some. All she has to do is make toffee in a pan, put the apples on to wooden sticks, and dip them in the toffee until they are coated all over. Then allow the toffee to set, and you have perfect toffee-apples.

While she is making the toffee-apples, your mum might as well help you with a practical joke! Simply select some round, apple-sized *potatoes*. Put them on to sticks (having peeled them first) and let her coat them with toffee so that they look just like the toffee-apples.

Keep them separate from the apples so that *you* know which is which, and the next time you have friends round, offer them one of your really delicious toffee-apples. You, of course, take a real toffee-apple, but give your friends the toffee-potatoes. They will be in for quite a shock when they take a nice big bite out of this juicy-looking confection!

Voodoo

You probably know that in some foreign countries the natives actually shrink human heads, and these can be bought as curiosities. You may have seen pictures of them. Fortunately we do not have head-hunters in this country, but *you* can create your very own shrunken head to astonish your friends.

All you need is a large cooking apple. If you are lucky enough to have an apple tree in your garden then you will probably be able to get some windfallen apples and make quite a collection of heads.

Choose an apple that isn't too round, and carve it into the shape of a human head by putting a face on to it. This doesn't need to look too realistic, but gouge out some eye sockets, some nostrils, and a slit for a mouth, and some ears.

Take your finished sculpture and put it somewhere warm. The bottom of an airing cupboard is fine, or high up on a window ledge in warm sunshine. Don't put it outside though, otherwise birds will peck at it and insects will swarm around it, and before you know where you are the apple will have disappeared altogether!

As the apple dries over a period of a week or two, you will find that it will begin to shrivel and shrink, and the face will take on a very realistic appearance. When you are satisfied with the way it looks, stick some crêpe hair or wool on the top to make it look like human hair. Now take your shrunken head to school in a box, telling your friends that your grandfather brought it back from the jungle during the war after he had escaped from cannibals!

Money making

You can catch anybody out with this.

You: There's only one way to make lots of money.
Victim: What's that then?
You: I might have known that *you* wouldn't know how!

You ape!

Get a book that is all about apes, monkeys, baboons or gorillas out of your local library, or school library. Or perhaps you have a book of your own on these particular creatures.

Take an ordinary looking-glass or vanity mirror, the small flat kind that ladies often carry in their handbags, and place it just inside the first page of the book. If it is your own book you could even glue the mirror to a blank page, or put it on with double-sided sticky tape or Blu-Tack.

You then lie your 'ape' book down on a table. When your victim comes into the room you say: 'I've found this marvellous book all about monkeys. It has some incredible pictures of apes in it. Have a look at this one on page one.'

Your victim will then open the book to the page you have told him, and will see himself staring back! You can really make a monkey out of somebody!

Mind-reading

Tell your victim that you are a great mind-reader, and even if she does a complicated sum in her head you will be able to say the answer.

Ask her to think of a number. Absolutely any number.

Now get her to double it.

Multiply it by five.

Add one hundred and one.

Finally, take away the number that she first thought of.

Remind her that you are such a wonderful mind-reader that you can easily say the answer. When she has done all her calculations you do just what you said you would and say: 'THE ANSWER!'

Blood bath

When you are feeling particularly kind and benevolent, tell your mother that you will run her a nice hot bath so that she can relax.

You go into the bathroom and you run the water, and get the towels ready, and the soap, bath salts, and so on. When the bath is ready, give her a call and then run and hide. She will walk into the bathroom and you will hear: 'Aaaaaaaagggghhhh! Screaaaaaaaaaaammmm!'

The bath will look as if it is full of blood. You have put just a few drops of red food colouring or cochineal in the water. All you need are a couple of drops and the water will go blood red.

Water torture

Having run mum a blood bath, offer to run your dad a nice relaxing bath too. Tell him that you promise not to put anything in the bath except pure water. That way he cannot possibly complain, can he?

Go into the bathroom and run the water, and get his bathrobe ready, and his towels, soap, and so on. When all is ready call him, and then run and hide.

When he arrives in the bathroom he will look at the bath and see that it is pure water with nothing added, just as you promised. He will leap into the bath. 'Aaaaaaaaaaaaaaaaaggggggggggghhhhhhhhhhh!'

You have filled the bath with COLD water! SERIOUS NOTE: Never play this practical joke using HOT water. This could be very dangerous.

Bounce! Bounce!

To astound passers-by in the street, especially if you are standing in a bus queue, all you need is a handkerchief and a bouncy rubber ball.

Place the ball in the centre of the handkerchief. Hold on to it through the handerkerchief and sew around it, so that the ball is held in a little pouch. If you cannot sew, or are not allowed to use a needle, then a small rubber band slipped over the handkerchief and the ball will keep it in place. Screw up the handkerchief and put it in your pocket.

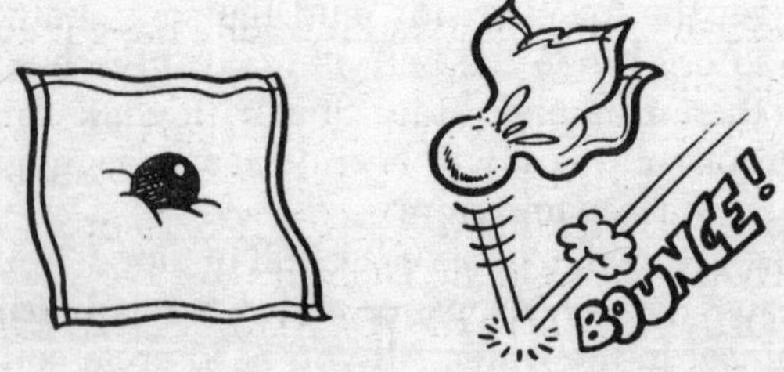

When you are amongst a group of people, take the handkerchief out of your pocket and pretend to blow your nose on it. Then throw the handkerchief to the ground – and it will bounce straight back into the air again! Catch it, put it back into your pocket, and carry on as if absolutely nothing had happened, as if bouncing handkerchiefs on the ground were a normal everyday occurrence!

Out of sight, out of mind

Take a 2p piece or a 10p piece, and show it to your friends. Now tell your victim that you are going to place the coin somewhere in the room where everyone else can see it, but you are going to hypnotise him so that he won't be able to see it however hard he looks.

Wave the coin in front of his eyes a couple of times

and then place it right on top of his head. Everyone will be able to see it but the victim!

Sleeping beauty

If one of your relations has a habit of falling asleep in a chair after meals or while watching television, and a lot of people do, there are a number of tricks that you can play on them. Here are four of the best!

1 If grandad or grandma drops off to sleep in a chair, or even your father or mother, make a little cardboard sign and gently lay it on their lap. If they are a very heavy sleeper you can even put a piece of string on it and carefully hang it around their neck.

Write something funny on the sign like:
SILENCE – MAN AT WORK or
BRITISH MUSEUM – EXHIBIT 6728 or
AWAITING COLLECTION or
FOUND ON LIVERPOOL STREET STATION
or even
THE ORIGINAL SLEEPING BEAUTY!

This will cause great amusement for anybody that happens to walk in the room, and always causes a great chuckle if your unfortunate victim happens to fall asleep in a deckchair in the garden where passers-by can see your sign. Your victim will wake up not realising that he or she has been a great source of amusement all the time.

2 If your father happens to fall asleep in a chair and still has shoes on, one of the simplest jokes is to tie his shoelaces together.

You will need to tug very, very gently on the laces first of all to get them undone. Once they are undone all you have to do is tie one shoelace from each shoe together in a bow. Do not tie them in a strong knot, just a simple bow will be sufficient to make your victim wonder why his feet won't move!

3 If your victim is a very heavy sleeper, then you can have lots of fun.

You can place a funny hat gently on their head, or cover them up with a sheet, or even tie their wrists with string to the arms of the chair! If your victim wears glasses, then carefully stick a few of those coloured sticky dots or stars that you can buy quite cheaply on to the lenses. When they wake up they will literally see spots or stars before the eyes!

4 One final practical joke for sleepers requires a bit of co-operation from the rest of the family. If everyone is willing to join in then you really can go to town and have tremendous fun.

What you do when your victim falls asleep after lunch is this: If it is about 2.00 pm in the afternoon, change all the clocks in the room to about 8.00 pm. Draw the curtains across so that it looks as if it is dark outside and put on a lamp or small light just as you would if it were evening. Stand a cold cup of tea beside the victim so that it looks as if it has been standing there for hours.

If you want to go even further, get the rest of the family to put on their nightclothes and dressing-gowns and make themselves cups of cocoa. You then all sit around the room just as if you were having your final bedtime drink. Start chatting amongst yourselves and your victim will slowly begin to wake up.

Immediately he will look at the clock, which by this time might say that it is half-past eight or even nine o'clock. He will then notice that it is dark and that you are all ready for bed, and quite naturally he will think that he has been asleep for hours and hours, not only missing his tea but all his favourite television programmes too! After a while you tell him that it is all a joke and that it is really only 3 o'clock in the afternoon!

Happy birthday!

Birthdays are not really the time for playing practical jokes because you don't want to spoil anyone's happy day. But this is one trick that you can play, for a while anyway. You will need the co-operation of the rest of the family.

All get up very early, while your victim is still in bed, and hide all the birthday cards that the postman has brought. Leave just a bill, or a nasty official-looking brown envelope on the mat.

When your victim gets up, say *absolutely nothing* about his or her birthday, but simply carry on as if it were a normal morning. He or she will notice that not one single birthday card has arrived. There will not be one single present, and nobody will have said 'happy birthday'. Just when your poor victim is looking really dejected, all burst into a rousing chorus of 'Happy Birthday to You' and shower him or her with presents, flowers and all the birthday cards, and prepare a really special breakfast just to show how much you care.

End of bananas

You: Did you know that they are not going to grow bananas any longer?
Victim: No, why is that?
You: Because they are long enough already!

Cheers!

If someone in your family likes to drink a glass of wine or spirits, then you can play a very good practical joke on them. Drinking too much can be bad for your health, so this could be a method of making them think seriously about how much they drink!

You need to plan ahead to play this joke. Every time a bottle is empty and it is put aside for the bottle bank, secretly take it to your bedroom and keep it hidden until you need it. When you want to use it, fill it with a liquid the same colour as the original drink that your victim expects to find inside. Here are some examples:

Gin or vodka

These two drinks are completely colourless and look just like plain tap water, which is exactly what you use. Fill the bottles with cold water and put them in the place of the full ones.

Red wine

Fill the bottle up with blackcurrant juice, or water that has been coloured with red food colouring or cochineal. Take care not to spill any of the food colouring or get it on your fingers as this will give the game away.

White wine

Just fill the bottle with ordinary cold water until it is about three-quarters full, and then top it up with cold tea. (Not tea that has milk in it, just plain tea.) You may find that you need a little more tea, or a little less, so you will need to experiment to get the correct shade. If you compare it with a real bottle of white wine you will be able to match the colour up. For wine bottles you might need to keep the cork, too, push it back firmly in the bottle once you have filled it so that it looks like a new bottle of wine.

Whisky or brandy

Keep the original empty whisky or brandy bottle

and again fill it with cold tea. You might find it easier if you put the tea in a jug and pour it into the bottle through a funnel, that way you won't spill any. If you are not using tea-bags, be sure to strain the tea well otherwise any tea leaves floating around in the bottle would really give the game away!

Whisky is a golden brown colour, brandy is slightly darker, so you may find that you want a stronger brew of tea. Again, it is wise to match your tea against a real bottle of whisky or brandy so that you get the exact colour match that you want. You might be able to get an adult or an older brother or sister to help you. They are sure to see that it is a very funny practical joke, and it will be much funnier too if *everybody* knows about it, except the poor victim!

Tonic water

A teaspoonful of liver salts to a bottle full of cold water will look just like tonic water. It is best to fill the bottle to about three-quarters full and then add the salts. Now screw the top on tightly. When your victim undoes it, it will fizz just like real tonic... but the taste, ugh!

The eleven-letter alphabet

We all know that the English alphabet contains twenty-six letters. The shortest alphabet in the whole world is the Hawaiian alphabet, which has just twelve letters. A practical joke to play on your friends is to tell them that there are just eleven letters in the alphabet.

Of course, nobody will believe you, so you prove it to them like this:

T	H	E		A	L	P	H	A	B	E	T
1	2	3		4	5	6	7	8	9	10	11

Weigh out

If you have a weight-conscious person in your household, then you can play a practical joke on them in the bathroom. All you need to do is alter the little dial on the bathroom scales to make them either gain or lose a few pounds.

Imagine your mother's or sister's surprise when she gets on the scales and discovers that she has gained sixteen stones in a week! Make sure that you know how to put the scales right again afterwards, otherwise you could end up in trouble. Usually you simply turn the dial so that the arrow starts at nought.

If you feel it would be unwise to touch your bathroom scales, and it might be better for your health if you don't, don't worry! You can still have fun. All you need is a metal ruler.

Hold it on a table or window ledge with one hand so that several inches overlap. You will find that if you tap the end that is sticking out with your finger, it will make a lovely boing sort of sound!

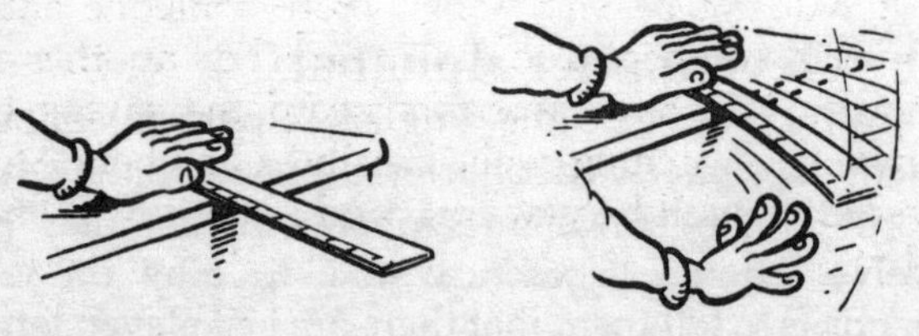

Wait outside the bathroom door and when you hear somebody getting on the scales – you can usually hear a clanking, whirring sound when somebody steps on them – simply give your ruler a flick and make a loud boing sound. Your victim will certainly think that she has broken the scales!

'My! You're putting on weight!' you say, when she emerges, red-faced, from the bathroom!

Hello! Hello!

The next time your mother has a bath, wait until you know that she is in the water. Then tip-toe outside and either ring the doorbell or rat-a-tat on the door-knocker. After a few minutes you pretend to open the door, and in a loud voice you say: 'Oh, hello Mrs Jones. How nice to see you. Yes, do come in, my mother will be so pleased to see you!'

Your mother will be sitting trembling in the bath, not daring to come out! For added fun, pretend that the person at the door is the one person your mother would least like to see at that particular time!

Yawn! Yawn!

A very good practical joke that you can play on a bus or underground train is actually one of the simplest, but most effective there is. All you have to do is yawn. Not just once, but a couple of times, with a few minutes in between.

It will not be very long before someone sitting opposite you begins to yawn too. Then another and another. You have probably heard the saying that yawning is catching, well, it really is, and before long everybody will be yawning, and nobody will know why!

Cheap food

Next time you are in a restaurant or café, there is a way of getting food quite cheaply! Your poor unfortunate victims might not approve, though. What you do is simply buy yourself a cup of tea or some other kind of drink, and allow your victim to buy a tasty sandwich.

You then say to him or her: 'I bet you 50p that I could eat that sandwich without letting it touch my lips, teeth or tongue.'

This claim sounds so absolutely impossible that your victim is certain to let you try and prove it. Whereupon you pick up the sandwich and take a great big bite out of it and start eating it in the normal way. Of course, your victim will shout that the food is touching your lips, teeth and tongue, so you say: 'Yes, it looks as if I lost my bet doesn't it? Here's 50p!'

You then hand over the money, which is very cheap for a sandwich!

Something hot

Being such a kind and generous person, you will be quite happy to make a tasty sandwich for your friend. But it will be a sandwich that he won't forget in a hurry! When you make the sandwich, include in it something that is very, very hot – some extra strong mustard, dried chillis, paprika pepper, or some tabasco sauce. Don't put it all over the sandwich, but just in one small area, so that your victim can begin eating without noticing that there is anything wrong.

Suddenly he will reach the hot part! Be standing by with a glass of iced water: he might need a long drink!

Something sweet

Having said how sorry you are about the hot sandwich, the very least you can do is offer your victim a delicious iced bun or cake. On the table you will have a plate of buns, each beautifully decorated with whipped cream and a cherry on the top.

Because they look so mouthwatering, your victim will certainly be tempted, and as he sees that you are eating one then he will take one for himself. If he chooses the bun himself from a plate, then there cannot be anything wrong with it. Can there?

Yes! Your bun is delicious because it is decorated with real whipped cream. The one your victim takes will look just as delicious but, yuk, what looks like cream is actually TOOTHPASTE! You take an ordinary plain bun and pipe a little toothpaste around it for decoration.

WARNING: Do not decorate the cake with shaving foam, or anything other than toothpaste. Toothpaste is *meant* to go in the mouth and will do no harm. Shaving foam or anything else could be very dangerous.

Black-eyed Susie!

Borrow some dark blue or dark grey eyeshadow from your mother, your sister, or a friend. Just before you come home from school, go into the cloakroom and smudge a little of this eyeshadow around one of your eyes and make it look as if you have a black eye.

You can then tell all your friends that you have just beaten the school bully in a fight. Imagine your mother's horror when you walk in sporting a nasty-looking black eye! Fetch the smelling salts!

You can use the eyeshadow to give yourself a few nasty-looking bruises on your arms and legs too!

Shut that door!

This is a practical joke that has been played by children for generations and is still very popular. All you need is a metre or two of string.

You also need two rooms that are quite close together, and that both contain unsuspecting victims. Bedroom doors are ideal, and you can try this joke soon after your victims have entered their

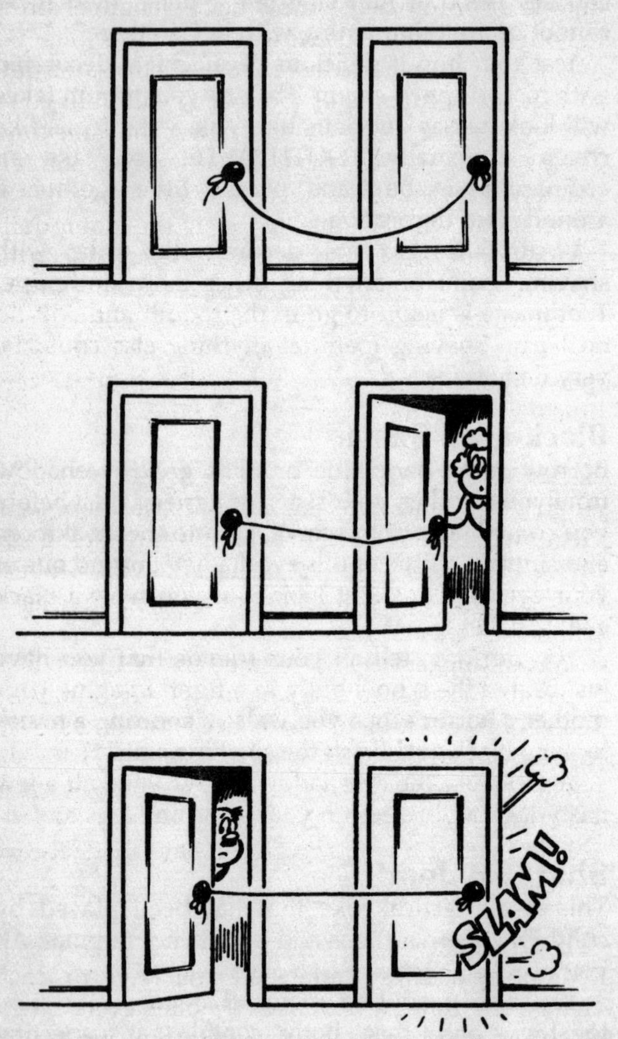
SLAM!

rooms, but before they have had time to get undressed or into bed. Simply tie the length of string to both door handles, leaving it fairly slack.

Now knock on both doors at exactly the same time so that the occupants of the rooms will both come and answer their doors at more or less the same time. The person that opens his or her door first (and it is unlikely that they will open their doors at exactly the same time) will be able to open the door quite normally, but as soon as the second person opens the door the string will pull the first door shut!

If the first person opens the door again it will pull the second person's door shut. They can carry on in this way for a long time, not realising why every time they open the door it shuts again!

Refreshing tea

After a hot sandwich and a toothpaste bun, your victim will certainly feel in need of a nice strong cup of tea. This you offer to make and you promise faithfully that you will add nothing to it, and that it will be just tea and milk.

You disappear into the kitchen and return with a cup and saucer of tea, carrying it very, very carefully. Tell your victim to sip it slowly because the kettle has just boiled and the drink is incredibly hot. He or she will lift the cup slowly and sip it gingerly so as not to get burnt.

Don't worry, it won't burn. You have made the tea with COLD water!

All change

To fool your entire family all you have to do is change the time of day. Secretly alter every single clock and watch in the house so that they are exactly one hour faster.

Having done this, do not say anything to anybody,

but continue about your business as if nothing has happened. Don't keep asking people what the time is either, otherwise this will make them suspicious. Sooner or later somebody will notice that it's much later than they thought it was, and think that perhaps the clock is wrong. They will go into another room and see that the clock in there says exactly the same time.

If someone suspects that the clocks might have gone wrong, you can offer to ring the Speaking Clock. When you do this you need only listen for a couple of minutes, then you can put the receiver down and tell them that the time is whatever you have changed the clock to.

But be careful the joke doesn't backfire, or you might get sent to bed an hour early!

Scar face!

To give yourself an unsavoury-looking scar or cut is quite an easy business. You might even have people fainting on the spot!

First, draw a thin red line on your hand with a lipstick, or a felt-tip pen if it is the kind that will wash off easily. Pinch the skin gently together where you have drawn your cut, and put a little Copydex on the crease. This is a rubbery glue which will peel off very easily. It is frequently used in the theatre for sticking on false beards and moustaches because it goes completely clear when dry and peels off painlessly. DO NOT USE ANY OTHER KIND OF GLUE.

When the Copydex is dry, let the skin go gently, and you will find that you have what looks like a nasty-looking scar on your hand. If you let a few drops of stage blood trickle down the groove it will look just like a recent cut, or you can draw a few black lines across the gash to look like stitches. Whatever you do, it will look *very* painful!

Butter-fingers!

Does your mother or father ever knock handles off cups when washing up? This can easily happen and more often than not the handle is knocked clean off, leaving no sharp edges.

If this does happen, see if you are allowed to keep the cup for practical jokes. Take a couple of small pieces of Blu-Tack, and put them on the ends of the handle. You will find that if you press the handle back on to the side of the cup, it will stick and you will not be able to see that it has ever been broken off. Put some water in the cup (but don't fill it), stand it on a saucer and give it to someone to drink. When they go to pick up the cup by the handle, it will come off in their hand, much to their surprise!

Kiss the book!

You: Do you see this book?
Victim: Yes, why?
You: I bet you that I can kiss it inside and outside without even opening it.
Victim: I bet you can't!
You: I bet you £100 I can.
Victim: OK, go on then.

All you do is kiss the book on the cover, then take it outside and kiss it again. You have kissed it inside and out, and you haven't opened it up! Now ask your victim for £100!

Invisible thread

Have a look in the needlework basket at home and see if there is any invisible thread. It is used for mending, and although it is extremely strong, it is practically colourless and single thread is rather like a very fine hair.

You will no doubt think of many uses to which

this thread can be put to play superb practical jokes. One of them is this: next time the table is laid for dinner, tie a long piece of invisible thread to someone's dessert spoon. Tie a button on the other end of the cotton so that you will be able to find the thread very easily. Trail the cotton across the table – as it is so fine nobody will see it – and let the button end hang over where you will sit yourself.

Halfway through the meal, with your hand under the table, very slowly pull on the cotton so that the person's spoon moves mysteriously across the table on its own. Make sure that the spoon has a clear path and doesn't knock over any glasses, or cause anything to spill. Watch the astonished look on the face of your victim. How can it be anything to do with YOU – you are at the opposite end of the table!

Magic marker

Tell your victim that you have a special magic pen. You say that whatever he writes with it, even if he writes a message in a different room, you will immediately be able to read in your mind what he has written. Give him the pen and a piece of paper and tell him to write a sentence. It can be as long or as short as he likes, but he must not let you see what he has written. Reassure him that whatever he writes with this pen, you will know.

Tell him to go into another room and write his message. While he is out of the room you run and hide, because your victim will discover that when he tries to write a sentence with the pen, he can't! You have removed the ink cartridge from it so that it will not write at all!

Come up and see me

Try this on one of your school friends:

If I lived up here...

...and you lived down here...

...would you come up and see me sometime?

Money making

Here is a money-making practical joke which rarely fails. All you need is an empty matchbox and a 20p piece. Show your victim the box and the coin. Place the 20p inside the box, close it up and rattle it around, just to prove that the coin is inside.

Now ask your victim to put a 20p piece in the box as well. This he or she will do, so there is now 40p in the box altogether. Your conversation should now go like this:

You: Forty pence is quite a lot of money, isn't it?
Victim: Yes.
You: You could buy a bar of chocolate or a comic with that. Would you like to make some money yourself?
Victim: Yes, of course.
You: Well, there's 40p in this matchbox. Will you give me 30p for it?

Your victim is sure to take up this offer because it seems like a good deal, and he will walk off quite happily feeling that he has gained 10p for nothing. The joke is that it is YOU who have gained the 10p. Victims always forget that one of the 20p pieces in the box was theirs already!

Shopping list

This is one of the oldest tricks in the book, but it still works every time. What you do is give somebody a shopping list, and ask them if they will just get you a couple of items and you will pay them when they return. Make sure that the shopping list is folded in half so that they do not look at it immediately.

When your victim reaches the shop, he or she will open up the list and might even begin looking around the shelves for the items. But they won't find any of them! Everything on your list will prove to be totally impossible to buy!

Here are the kind of items you might have on your shopping list:

> 1 pint of gravy
> 1 litre of tartan paint
> ½ dozen pig's eggs
> 1 packet of hot ice-cream
> a left-handed hammer
> round sugar cubes
> 1 pot of white ink

Warning!

You: Look out! There's a henweigh on the back of your neck.
Victim: What's a henweigh?
You: Oh, about three pounds.

Indian chief

You: I can turn you into a Red Indian.
Victim: How?
You: See, it works?

Thanks a lot

The next time a friend of yours, or a member of your family, has a birthday, why not give them a special present? You walk into the room with a very large parcel. When your victim takes off the first layer of paper, underneath will be another layer. Then another layer. Then another. And another. And another. And another. And another. And another. And another. And another. Half an hour, and twenty layers of paper later, our victim will eventually reach...an old potato!

You now give your friend the *real* present, which has one layer of paper on it! With the first parcel the more layers you can put on it, the better. If you run out of wrapping paper, use newspaper instead.

Sock it to me

Take your victim's socks and carefully, but loosely, sew along the top of them so that he is unable to get his feet inside. If you stitch them up and then roll the socks up into a ball, when your victim comes to put them on he will wonder why he cannot find the right end. DO NOT try this joke with girls' tights, though, as this will tear and damage them and you will be very unpopular!

What would you do?

You: If you were walking down a narrow country lane, which had no trees to climb and no holes to hide in and you didn't have a gun and there wasn't a soul about to help you, and you saw a great fierce grizzly bear coming towards you, what would you do?
Victim: Run.
You: What, with a bear behind?!

Ouch!

To pretend that you have a really nasty bump on your arm, take a marble and stick it to your arm with a piece of sticking plaster, and then cover the whole arm with a bandage. If you put several marbles down one arm you can pretend that some horrible insect has just bitten you. Or you can say that you have been attacked by a swarm of flies. The sticking plaster will prevent the marbles from rolling about under the bandage.

For a horrible-looking bump on your forehead, simply place a small wad of cotton wool under a large piece of sticking plaster. My goodness! What have you done to your head?

Strings attached

Tie a cup on a door knob exactly like this:

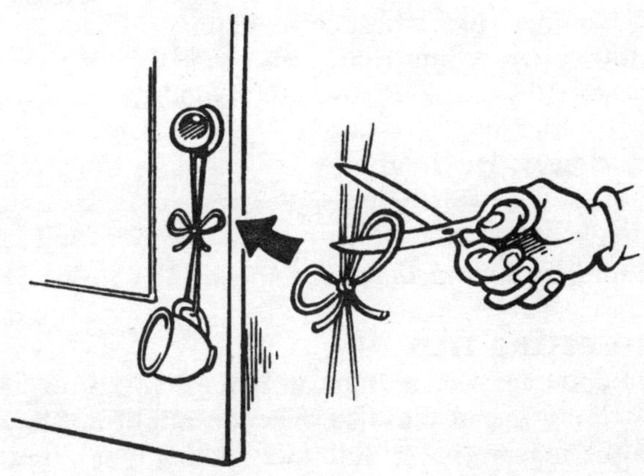

Now give your victim a pair of scissors and challenge him to cut the string *without* letting the cup fall to the floor, and *without* touching the cup. You can bet him any amount of money you like because he won't dare do it!

When he has given up, take the scissors from him and cut the string. BUT you cut one of the loops in half. This way you have cut the string, but the cup will not fall. Clever!

Clangers!

Gather together as many small pieces of metal as you can – keys, pencil sharpeners, curtain rings, whistles, tin lids, and so on. Keep them all together in a safe place until you need them.

One day offer to dry the dishes for your mother. If she has been the butt of many of your practical jokes, tell her that it is about time she had a rest from all the everyday chores and allow her to put her feet up for once and have a nice cup of tea. You go into the kitchen and start to do the washing up. When all is quiet drop all your little pieces of metal on to the floor with a loud crash. You then gasp and say; 'Oh no! That was Mum's best china plate.'

Mother will come flying into the kitchen to see what you have broken now. FOOLED YA!

Fire down below!

You: Hey! Your shirt tail's on fire!
Victim: Is it?
You: (*pulling your victim's shirt tail out*) It's out now!

Man-eating fish

Have you ever seen a man eating fish? You probably have, quite recently in fact, but you might not have thought anything of it. Tell your friends that in your dining-room you keep a man-eating fish. Nobody will believe you, of course. So, just to prove it, you take them in and show them your father eating a plate full of haddock! It really is a man eating fish!

Carrot tops

Has your mother ever complained that you don't wash your ears properly? Has she ever said that you'll end up with carrots growing out of your ears? If so, get some green leaves from the tops of some carrots, keep them in your bedroom and place them in your ears one morning just before your mother comes in to wake you up!

Ghosts in the night

If you want to make your parents think that there is a ghost in the house, all you need is a reel of cotton and an ordinary sheet of paper.

Just before your parents go to bed at night you can prepare this practical joke. With a piece of adhesive tape, attach the cotton to the sheet of paper, and lay the piece of paper on the top of the wardrobe where it is out of sight.

Trail the cotton down behind the wardrobe, along the skirting board, under the door and into your own bedroom. When your parents go into their room they will not notice anything at all. Allow them ten minutes to get into bed, or wait until you see that their light has gone out. Now start to make low wailing noises like a demented ghost, and at the same time give your piece of cotton just a very gentle tug. This will cause the piece of paper to float down off the wardrobe, making an eerie rustling noise as it lands on the bed. Your parents will disappear under the sheets with fright and won't dare come out to investigate!

Live ghosts

To scare your family in the night, dress up as a ghost yourself. All you need is an old sheet with a couple of holes for your eyes cut out of it. Make sure that it is an old sheet that nobody wants, and do get permission before you start cutting holes in it.

Put on your ghost costume in secret and then come out and haunt people. Everyone expects to see ghosts on Hallowe'en, October 31st, so if you do it then nobody will be frightened – but put it on when it is July 14th or September 3rd or March 5th and you *will* scare people.

A-tissue!

During the hay-fever season, or when a lot of people have colds, investing in a box of tissues can be well worthwhile if you want to play a practical joke. When you get the box of tissues home, take them all out of the box very carefully. Now put a dab of glue on each tissue and join it to the next one so that all the tissues are attached together in one long string. The kind of glue that comes in the form of a stick is ideal for this because you do not get in a mess and you only need just a very tiny amount of glue on each tissue.

Return the tissues to the box in the same order, so that it looks like a normal box of tissues. Leave the box lying around. When your victim is about to sneeze he will reach for a tissue and instead of one he or she will end up with fifty in a string!

Round the bend

Here is a practical joke that you can play on passers-by in the street, and you won't fail to catch them out. All you need is a very long tape measure, the kind that is used to measure race tracks or playing fields. You can probably borrow one from your games teacher at school. If you cannot get hold of a tape measure then a length of string, about 10 metres long, will do just as well.

Go out into the street and wait by the corner of a building. When you see a likely victim coming along, stop them. Say that you are doing a project for school and would they be so kind as to help you for a few minutes. Tell them that you have got to measure the nearby building. Give them one end of the string, and get them to stand and hold it.

You walk off around the corner and when you are out of sight, you stop another passer-by. Say that you are doing a project for the school and would they help you measure this building. Yes, the same old story. When they are holding the *other* end of the string, you disappear to a spot where you can watch both your victims, but they are unable to see you. This is where the fun starts! Sooner or later one or both of your victims will get impatient and will walk round the corner to find out just what is going on!

It might be best to use a piece of string rather than a tape measure, because if you use the measure you will have to go and get it back from them, whereas you can abandon the piece of string and run!

Ink blots

Spill a few drops of ink on to a sheet of blotting paper and allow them to dry. You can speed this up by putting the blotting paper somewhere warm.

When it is dry, cut around the blots, and you will have your own ink blots. Leave them around the house or next to an empty ink bottle!

Get dressed!

Get up early one morning, before your mother comes in to wake you up. Get dressed and ready for school, and then put your pyjamas back on again over the top of your clothes and return to bed and pretend to be asleep. Now just wait in bed until someone comes in to get you up. Your mother will think that you are going to be late for school. You open your eyes blearily when she comes into the room.

You: What time is it, Mum?

Mum: Time you were up! You're going to be late for school.
You: No, I won't. I can get dressed in ten seconds.
Mum: Don't talk silly.
You: I can, Mum. Go outside and I bet you 50p I'll be out and dressed in 10 seconds.

Your mother has hardly got outside the door before you appear fully dressed and ready for school – and demanding your 50p!

Cut finger

If you want to get out of playing games or doing the washing up, or tidying your room, then what better than to have a badly cut finger that is all bandaged up. All you need to do is get a piece of cardboard and make a tube out of it so that it fits easily on to your finger. Now glue some bandage around the cardboard tube, and paint on a bit of red 'blood' for effect. You now have a ghastly-looking bandaged finger that you can slip on and off your hand whenever you want.

To make it look even more painful, you can make five of these, one for each finger of your right hand! To make it look worse still, bend a small sliver of wood or a piece of cocktail stick into an 'L' shape and slip it under the bandage so that it looks like a very nasty splinter sticking out. Ouch!

I know what

Take a piece of paper and write the word 'WHAT' on it in large letters, and fold the paper up into four. Put the piece of paper into your pocket and go up to your victim.

You: I know what you are going to say next.
Victim: What?

You produce the piece of paper from your pocket and show it to him.

You: You see, I knew exactly what you were going to say!

Practical pests

A lot of people do not like creepy-crawlies, such as spiders or caterpillars, and would have a surprise if they found one in an unexpected place. With the help of a few pipe cleaners you can put some in unexpected places!

Caterpillars can be made by cutting a length of pipe cleaner about 2cm long. Dip the pipe cleaner into some green paint and allow it to dry. You now have something that looks just like a real caterpillar. Pop one into somebody's shoe, or bed, or even into a nice green salad that your victim is about to eat.

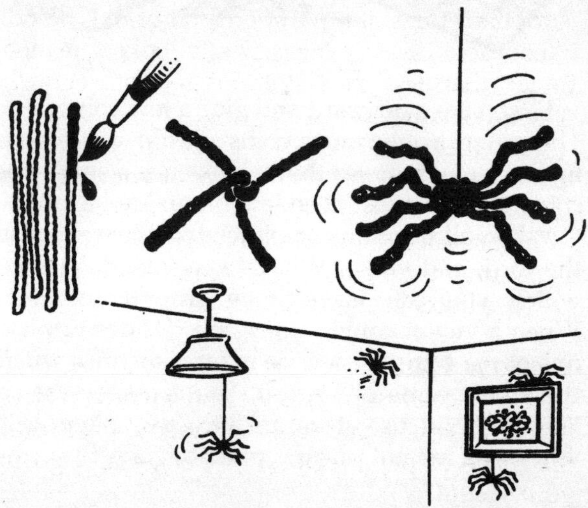

A spider can be made by painting four pipe cleaners black and twisting them around each other to make them look like a spider's legs. Where the pipe cleaners all join in the middle will provide the body. With a piece of invisible thread, hang the spider from a lampshade, or from the curtains, or even hang it over something and keep hold of the other end of the string so that your spider will descend when you let go of the thread.

Stop thief!

This is a practical joke that will prove how honest people are – and help you catch a thief if he tries to steal any money from you!

First, take a postcard and glue a few coins on to it. Then glue a few more coins on top of these, and finally a few more so that it looks like a small pile of coins that have just been laid down haphazardly.

When all the coins are stuck together, cut around the card, and you will have a realistic pile of coins which you can leave lying around somewhere. When a victim comes along and decides to pick up one of the coins, he will be in for a surprise when all the others come up with it! You can keep the coins like this and use it as an attractive paperweight, when you are not playing practical jokes!

Funny drawers

To give someone a surprise when they open a drawer, simply take out the top drawer of a chest of

drawers or dressing-table. Carefully remove everything that is inside the drawer and store it in a box for safe keeping. Turn the drawer upside down so that the bottom of the drawer is now at the top, and put it back where it came from.

When your victim opens the drawer to put some thing inside they will wonder why they can't get anything in!

Money from the sky

Your victim is walking along the road. There is nobody about. Suddenly money starts falling from the sky! Are they really pennies from heaven? She will begin to wonder!

The secret is that YOU are hidden behind a nearby wall or fence, and you throw a 1p coin into the air so it lands at your victim's feet. At first she will probably think that it has fallen from her pocket and she will start looking for a hole. Then clang! Another coin falls from the sky. She might pick this one up, too. But then yet another falls. You can have a lot of fun with this because of the very puzzled look on your victim's face. She just will not be able to work out where the money is falling from.

This may seem like an expensive joke, but for just 20p you can throw twenty pennies and get a lot of laughs into the bargain.

Cactus caper

If you want to play a practical joke on one of your teachers, this is the one that is certain to catch them out. You can plan this joke in advance by telling your teacher a few days before about your mother's very unusual hobby of collecting and growing all different kinds of cacti. Tell the teacher that your mother has varieties from all over the world. Say that you will get your mother to send one along as a present.

A couple of days later you turn up with the cactus for the teacher. It is in fact a small green pan scrubber or pot scourer, the prickly kind that you can buy very cheaply in any supermarket. Stand the pot scourer in a small flower pot of real earth and it will look just like a variety of cactus. Unless your teacher knows a lot about plants she will be watering this one for months and not realise what it is!

WARNING: Do not try this joke on your biology teacher! Otherwise you could end up staying in after school writing 100 lines: 'I must not play practical jokes on my teachers.'

On the very last day of term, or when you leave the school altogether, *then* you can tell your teacher the truth!

Knock, knock

This is not a normal 'knock, knock' joke! You can play this joke when you are next having a meal or a drink with friends. Pick up your glass of lemonade, water, tea, milk, or whatever it is you might be drinking, and say to your friends: 'I bet you I can knock this cup of drink on the floor without spilling any of it.'

Nobody will believe that you can do this, and they are certain to ask you to have a go, because they will love to see you make a fool of yourself by spilling your drink all over the floor. You won't, of course!

All you do is get down on the floor and tap your cup gently on the ground a couple of times. There! You have knocked your drink on the floor, but you haven't spilt any of it!

Horrible handshake

During the winter months when it is cold enough to wear a scarf and gloves, you can shake hands with your friends and give them a really horrible handshake. Take off one of your gloves and stuff four of the fingers with newspaper, leaving the middle finger empty. Now push a wooden rod into the glove so that the end of the rod forms the middle finger. Finally stuff the rest of the glove with paper so that it looks just like a real hand. The rod should stick out of the end of the glove like this:

You can now hold on to the rod and keep your hand hidden up your sleeve so that the glove looks like your own hand. Now when you shake hands with someone they will grasp this stuffed glove. Aaaaaaaggghhh!

Eggsiting!

Offer to cook the family breakfast one morning. Tell them not to worry because you are only going to do something very simple like boiled eggs.

After about five minutes give them a call. As the family arrive in the kitchen they will see that you are eating a delicious boiled egg. Hungrily they will sit down to eat theirs, but when they crack them open they are going to be in for a surprise, because their eggs will not be quite the same as yours!

The last time you had boiled eggs you will have kept the shells, having washed and dried them carefully. When placed in egg cups, upside down, they will look just like real eggs – and these are what you use for your joke. You can either leave them empty or, if you are more adventurous, you can fill them with white marshmallows, or cold rice pudding. Anything that looks like an egg white at first glance until your victims put their spoons in!

Dark problem

Try this on one of your school friends:

You: Take any number.
Add two.
Subtract three.
Now close your eyes.
Dark, isn't it!

Up she goes!

This joke can be played at parties, or you can try it out amongst your friends. You need a couple of accomplices to help you out with it.

Get your victim to stand on a chair or small stool. Blindfold him or her. You and your accomplices stand around the chair. Rest your hand on the back of the chair, and get your accomplices to stand on either side with their hands resting on the seat. Your victim must place his or her hands on the shoulders of the two accomplices who are standing on either side of the chair.

Tell your victim that you are going to lift the chair up into the air. You and your two accomplices now bend your knees, and your blindfolded victim will feel as if the chair has been lifted several feet off the ground, and will start to feel very unsafe indeed. You now invite your victim to jump off the chair or stool, but of course they won't dare do that, firmly believing that they are now really high up in the air! You then stand up and remove the blindfold, showing them that they haven't moved an inch!

Crazy practical jokes

Show your victim this book. But don't show him what is inside, otherwise he might start playing tricks on you! Tell him that this is such an incredible book that you can lay it down on the floor and he won't be able to jump over it.

He won't believe you, so you challenge him to jump over it. You lay the book down on the floor in the *corner* of the room. Watch him try to jump over it now!

Get out of that!

If you really want to get your victim into a situation where she dare not move an inch, then this is the joke for you. Take care, however, where you do it otherwise you could end up with a mess on the floor.

Tell your victim that you are going to show her something really amazing. Take a paper cup of water and a stick which is long enough to reach up to the ceiling. Climbing on to a chair you position the cup of water against the ceiling and hold it in place with the stick. Ask your victim if she will just hold on to the stick for a second while you get down off the chair. Once she is holding the stick, you run across to the other side of the room, taking the chair with you.

You can now call her anything you like, because she won't dare move. As soon as she does the water will fall on her head!

WARNING: Don't play this joke in a room where the water might damage a carpet!

Library laughs

The next time you are at a friend's house, have a look at the books on his bookshelf. If he has a number of hardback books with loose covers you can have a bit of fun. The next time he goes out of the room, take some of the books off the shelf and carefully remove the covers. Now jumble the covers around and put them back on the wrong books. Return the books to the shelf, if possible keeping them in the same positions from which they were removed so that he doesn't notice that you have touched them.

He may not notice anything for some time, not until he takes one of his books off the shelf and cannot understand why his book about cars is now full of pictures of aeroplanes, and his book of planes has pictures of farmyard animals!

Ring! Ring! Ring!

Imagine that the next time your telephone rings, your mother or father goes to answer it and on lifting the receiver discovers that it continues ringing... and they can't stop it!

This is an easy practical joke to play, and all you need is a small strip of adhesive tape. If you can get hold of the 'invisible' kind it will be even better, but if you can't then ordinary sticky tape will do.

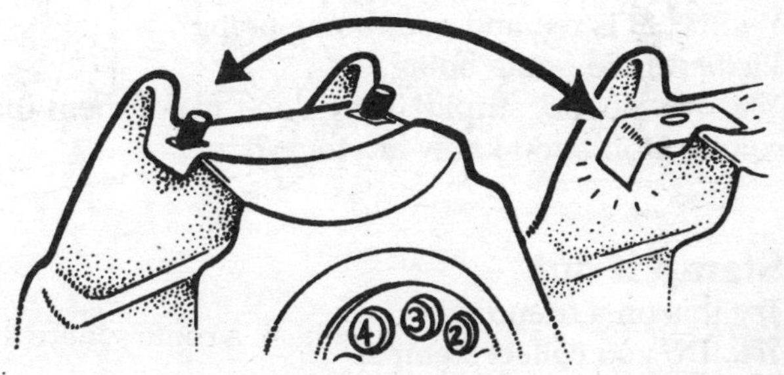

When nobody is looking, lift the telephone receiver and you will see two little knobs that pop up every time the receiver is lifted. All you need to do is tape one of these down carefully so that they do not rise when someone picks up the receiver. You need only tape one of them down because they work together.

When you have done this, simply replace the receiver and wait for the phone to ring. If you are really impatient you can dash out to a telephone box or to your friend's house and ring your number, but that way you will miss all the fun! When the telephone does ring, whoever answers the phone will pick up the receiver and say: 'Hello... hello... hello!' and it will be several seconds before they realise that the telephone is still ringing – and they will not be able to work out why!

Boing! Boing!

You: What is green and goes boing boing?
Victim: A green boing boing!
You: Quite right. Well done. Now, what is black and goes boing boing?
Victim: A black boing boing.
You: What is yellow and goes boing boing?
Victim: A yellow boing boing.
You: What is white and goes boing boing?
Victim: A white boing boing.
You: What is red and goes boing boing?
Victim: A red boing boing.
You: No, no, no, stupid! They don't make them that colour. Don't you know anything?!

Stamp it out

Try this on a friend.
You: Do you collect stamps?
Victim: Yes, I do.
You: Well, here's one for your collection!
And stamp on his foot! WARNING: DON'T STAMP ON YOUR FRIENDS FOOT TOO HARD! It is not meant to hurt.

If your friend says that he doesn't collect stamps, don't worry, there's a way around it! You simply say: 'Well, you ought to, it's a very interesting hobby. Here's a stamp to start you off!'

Another joke involving stamps, real stamps this time, is to cut an ordinary used stamp from the corner of an envelope and carefully decorate it with felt-tip pens. You then tell your stamp-collecting friends that you have an extremely rare stamp, and you will give it to them for their collection. When they have had it in their album for about six months, tell them the truth!

Sleep tight

For this joke you will need to be able to sew, although it will not matter if you cannot sew very well. You will also need a needle and some thread, plus your victims pyjamas or nightdress.

With the needle and cotton very loosely sew up the bottom of the trouser legs of your victim's pyjamas, or sew up the armholes of someone's nightdress.

Do not make the stitches too tight, otherwise they will be spotted by the victim before he or she puts the garment on. The fun comes when you watch the victim wriggling about on the floor, all tangled up in the sewn-up nightclothes.

Through the keyhole

You: I bet you that I can push myself through a keyhole.

Victim: I bet you can't!

You: I bet you £100 I can!

Victim: Go on then!

You then take a tiny piece of paper and write the word 'MYSELF' on it. Push the piece of paper through the keyhole and you have done exactly what you said you would do! You should now be £100 better off!

Itch-scratch-itch

A classic practical joke is one of putting itching powder down somebody's back. This is an unpleasant joke, and should not be played on anyone who has a sensitive skin, or anyone who is not going to be able to have a shower or a bath for several hours.

Itching powder can be bought cheaply in any joke shop, but you can make your own from the hips of the dog rose which grows wild in the countryside and is free. If you open up the hip, inside you will see a fluffy substance. Keep this in an envelope until you need it. Drop just a little down somebody's back and it will not be long before they start scratching.

T-time

You: The longest word in the dictionary is ANTIDIESTABLISHMENTARIANISM.
How many 'T's are there in that?
Victim: Three or four?
You: No, just two. T, h, a, t!

Throw your voice

Tell your friends that you are a ventriloquist and able to throw your voice. You sit down on a chair with your dummy, which can be any old doll or toy and you ask it questions. It answers back! Nobody can see your lips move, either!

The secret is that you have an ACCOMPLICE hidden under a table or behind the curtains, and HE is the dummy's voice!

Don't touch!

Show your victim the palm of your hand. Explain to him that in the centre of your hand is a brand-new baby. Say that it is very very tiny, and is now fast asleep. Point to the exact spot on your hand where the baby is lying. Explain that because the baby is so small and new, everyone has got to be extra specially careful with it. They say, touching the centre of your palm each time:

Daddy says: 'Don't touch they baby!'
Mummy says: 'Don't touch they baby!'
Brother says: 'Don't touch they baby!'
Sister says: 'Don't touch they baby!'
Grandma says: 'Don't touch they baby!'
Grandpa says: 'Don't touch they baby!'
Auntie says: 'Don't touch they baby!'
Uncle says: 'Don't touch they baby!'

You now ask your victim: 'Where is the baby?' He will point to the centre of your palm. As he does so you smack his hand and say: 'DON'T TOUCH THE BABY!'

Who's that?

The next time you have to telephone your parents, a relation, or even your best friend, try to disguise your voice so that they do not know who it is on the other end. You can play all kinds of jokes on them Tell them that you are from the water board and that no lavatories must be used for the next two weeks! Pretend that you are the Queen who has inadvertently been given a wrong number, or ask to speak to the Prime Minister.

If you can change your accent, or do impersonations, then you can have lots of fun. If you are no good at changing your voice, don't worry. Simply place a handkerchief over the mouthpiece of your telephone receiver and this will alter the way your voice sounds at the other end. Even your own mother won't recognise you!

Ripping time

Place a fifty pence piece on the ground and pretend that you haven't seen it. Position yourself so that you are close enough to the coin to keep your eye on it and so retrieve it when necessary, otherwise this could turn into a very costly joke.

When somebody comes along and bends down to pick up the coin, tear a piece of paper behind your back so that it makes a lovely ripping sound. Your victim will think that he has split his trousers!

Experiment with different pieces of paper to find the one that makes the best ripping sound. You will find that thicker paper, such as cartridge paper, often makes a good sound, as do tracing and greaseproof papers. Finally, offer your victim a safety pin, while you bend down to pick up your 50p!

What is it?

You: What is black and white and red all over?
Victim: That's easy! A newspaper.
You: Wrong! A skunk with nappy rash!

Remember me

You: Will you remember me in fifty years?
Victim: Yes.
You: Will you remember me in twenty-five years?
Victim: Yes.
You: Will you remember me in fifteen years?
Victim: Yes.
You: Will you remember me in ten years?
Victim: Yes.
You: Will you remember me in five years?
Victim: Yes.
You: Will you remember me in one year?
Victim: Yes.
You: Will you remember me next year?
Victim: Yes.
You: Will you remember me next month?
Victim: Yes.
You: Will you remember me next week?
Victim: Yes.
You: Will you remember me tomorrow?
Victim: Yes.
You: Will you remember me in an hour?
Victim: Yes.
You: Will you remember me in another minute?
Victim: Yes.
You: Knock, knock.
Victim: Who's there?
You: See, you've forgotten me already!

Sleep tight

As a final bedtime practical joke, take several newspapers. Separate the sheets of paper and roll them up into small balls. Next, take the pillow from your victim's bed. Take off the pillow case and hide the pillow under the bed so that it is completely out of sight. Now fill the pillow case with the balls of newspaper so that it looks just like the pillow and put it back on the bed. Your victim will not notice anything until he has put out the light and lays his or her head on the pillow. Crunch! Sweet dreams!

ATTACHED TO THE OTHER SIDE OF THIS PAGE IS A NICE NEW £5 NOTE

TURN THE PAGE VERY CAREFULLY SO THAT IT DOESN'T FALL OUT.

SORRY! YOU WEREN'T CAREFUL ENOUGH . . .

THE NOTE FELL OUT AGES AGO!

CRAZY WORLD RECORDS

THE MADCAP BOOK OF AMAZING RECORDS — AND THAT'S NO JOKE!

INTRODUCTION

I'm a record breaker.

Don't misunderstand me. I don't go around smashing up juke boxes and jumping on record players. Far from it. The records I break are world records of a very different kind. For example:

. . . I made the world's longest ever after-dinner speech when I talked non-stop for 11 hours on 13 and 14 February 1978!

. . . I have tossed the world's tiniest pancake – measuring 2 mm in diameter!

That's pretty impressive, I am sure you'll agree, but even though I am a record breaker you won't find any of my achievements listed in the pages that follow. That's because when I broke all my records I was getting on a bit and this book is all about the remarkable achievements of people aged between 0 and nineteen.

I am happy to say that CRAZY WORLD RECORDS is the most extraordinary collection of records on record – many of them records established by children and young people hundreds of years ago, many of them records that are more recent, and a lot of them records you might want to have a go at breaking yourself. Please remember though that before you attempt to break any record of any kind you must be sure to check with your parents (or guardians) that whatever it is you have in mind is really safe and meets with their approval.

Good luck!

MEET ROBERT WADLOW

Robert Pershing Wadlow, born in Alton, Illinois, USA, on 22 February 1918, became the tallest person in the history of the world. When he was 5 years old he was 5 feet 4 inches tall (1.62 m).

Henry VI of England became king when he was aged 269 days.

On 11 August 1980, 16 year old John Arnell played 8 musical instruments at the same time (4 percussion and 4 melodic).

On 19 March 1971, 11 year old Pamela Jackson of Tonbridge, Kent played 'God Save The Queen' on a piano using her toes.

On Saturday 4 April 1981, 10 year old Fenella Palmer acted as bridesmaid at a wedding for the 21st time. This time it was her sister Barbara's wedding.

The great German poet Goethe wrote a story in 7 languages when he was 10 years of age.

In 1958, Joy Foster became the youngest international champion of any sport by winning the Jamaican table tennis singles and mixed doubles when she was 8 years old.

Between 18 and 28 July 1968, six boys aged 13 to 15 took part in a Marathon Relay in Buttermere, Westmorland, covering 300 miles (482 km) in 230 hours 39 minutes.

In 1932 Magdalena College became the youngest competitor ever to represent Britain in the Olympic Games at just 11 years and 2 weeks old.

Carolyn Wharton of Texas, USA, is the youngest person ever to have been kidnapped. She was born at 12.46 pm on 19 March 1955, and at 1.15 pm she was kidnapped by a woman disguised as a nurse. Carolyn was 29 minutes old.

In 1431, Joan of Arc became the youngest person ever to be burnt at the stake. She was just 19 years old.

The composer Mozart gave a concert when he was 6.

George Filby, at the age of 8, rocked a rocking-chair non-stop for 100 hours.

In 1971, Stephen Newman, aged 12, completed 11,052 jumps on his pogo stick.

In 1965, Chick Linster, aged 16, of the USA, did 6,006 press-ups in 3 hours 54 minutes.

The poet Tennyson wrote a 6000 word poem when he was 10.

Dave Smith and Peter Dilley, two schoolboys, completed an egg and spoon marathon of 32 km (20 miles) in 5 hours 25 minutes in 1969.

Clifford Pearce, an English schoolboy, once ate 1,220 cold baked beans with a cocktail stick in 30 minutes.

At 22 months old, Elias Daou of Ghana was one of the world's largest babies. He was 91 cm (35¾ inches) in circumference and weighed 27.9 kilograms (61 pounds 8 ounces).

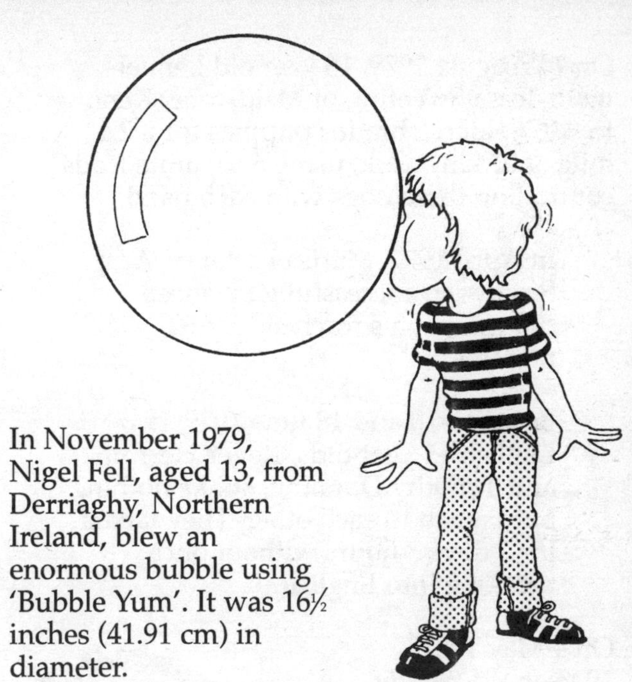

In November 1979, Nigel Fell, aged 13, from Derriaghy, Northern Ireland, blew an enormous bubble using 'Bubble Yum'. It was 16½ inches (41.91 cm) in diameter.

5 year old Patricia Edmunds of Exeter, Devon, on 15 February 1981, recited the Lord's prayer 132 times in succession.

Keep-fit fanatic Terence Wilkins was born on 19 April 1966. At the age of 13, on 21 April 1979, he did 1008 press-ups without stopping.

Using a 9 iron golf club, 16 year old Russell Cleveland of Swanage, Dorset, hit a standard table-tennis ball a distance of 103 metres (338 feet).

On 14 August 1979, 16 year old kennel-maid Tessa Sweeting of Maidstone, Kent, took 6 golden labrador puppies for a 2½ mile (4.02 km) walk, using 6 separate leads controlling three dogs with each hand.

In April 1972, Martin Foster of West Bromwich successfully balanced 3 oranges on his forehead for 92 minutes.

Between 10 and 18 June 1979, two English 15 year olds, Roger Herring and Timothy Dunning, spoke nothing but French to each other. They talked for 7 days 3 hours without once breaking into English.

On 4 May 1981, 10 year old Wendy Graham from Romford, Essex, cleaned her teeth continuously for 2 hours 27 minutes.

At the age of 7, Avril Broadbent of Sydney, Australia, had hair that reached to her ankles.

On 7 March 1976, Peter Worcester and Brian Thompson, both aged 9, kicked a football backwards and forwards to each other continuously for 10 hours, averaging 1 kick every 20 seconds.

Thomas Ingoldsby of Waterbeach, Cambridgeshire, at the age of 14, grew a fingernail on the little finger of his left hand that was 7½ inches (19.05 cm) long in January 1975.

From 9 to 12 August 1980, when aged 13 years 7 months, roller skating fanatic Kevin Harley of Bournemouth wore his skates for a total of 67 hours 37 minutes.

In January 1980, Gabriella Derwent, aged 9 years 7 months, played the violin non-stop for a total of 36 hours.

By August 1980, when he was 2½ years old, Michael Faulkner had visited over 30 different countries in his short life.

Anna Maria Porter, born in 1781, had her first novel published when she was 11 years old.

The 10th President of the United States, John Tyler, entered the College of William and Mary in 1802 when he was 12 years old.

The girls of Zimmerman Hall School and the boys of Ellsworth Hall in Michigan, USA, once talked to each other on the telephone for 691 hours 6 minutes.

Beethoven composed 3 piano sonatas when he was 13.

In 1888, an un-named American girl, aged 15, yawned non-stop for five weeks.

When he was 8 years old, Robert Wadlow was 6 feet (1.82 metres) tall.

Denis and David Goodwin are twins, but were born 56 days apart and in different years. Denis was born on 16 December 1952 and David was born on 10 February 1953.

A teenager called Alexandra Boyd of Perth, Australia, read 100,000 words per minute. In half an hour before a school examination she read *Wuthering Heights* by Emily Brontë, *Hamlet* by William Shakespeare, and several short stories.

Four boys of Central Grammar School, Birmingham, in 1972, played darts continuously for 150 hours.

14 year old Melvin Roberts of Lincoln ate nothing but baked beans. He averaged 14 tins a week, drinking only lemonade.

Kum Ung-Yong of Korea has an I.Q. of 210. At the age of 4 years 8 months he composed poetry, spoke Korean, English, German and Japanese and demonstrated the application of integral calculus.

Robert Schultz of Chicago was born at 5.14 pm on 14 June 1974 in the 14th year of his parents' marriage. His mother was born on 14 June 1937, and her mother was born 14 September 1903.

In 1938, a baby girl was born in St. George's Hospital, Hyde Park, London. She had 14 fingers and 12 toes.

Gale Klaine of West Palm Beach, USA, was born on 8 February 1957. Her father was born on 8 February 1912, and her grandmother was born on 8 February 1882.

David Morgan of Scarborough swam across the English Channel when he was 13.

King George IV was created Earl of Chester when he was 7 days old.

On 15 May 1475, Richard, Duke of York, received a knighthood at the age of 2 years 9 months. It is believed that he was murdered in the Tower of London with his brother in 1483.

Albert Einstein was 18 when he first proposed his famous theory of relativity.

Thomas Young, an eighteenth century physicist and Egyptologist, was able to speak twelve different languages by the time he was 8.

The author John Stuart Mill began to learn Greek when he was 3.

Handel composed a Mass when he was 13.

Henry V was 15 when he fought at the Battle of Shrewsbury in 1403.

Angel Bustamonte, on 17 December 1977, aged 18, performed 26,000 sit-ups without bending his knees once. It took 11 hours 45 minutes.

On 6 December 1977, 11 year old Anita Jokiel became the youngest international gymnast when she took part in a competition at Brighton.

In 1974, Scott Spencer aged 13, of Delaware, USA, jumped 6 miles (9.65 km) on a pogo stick in 6½ hours.

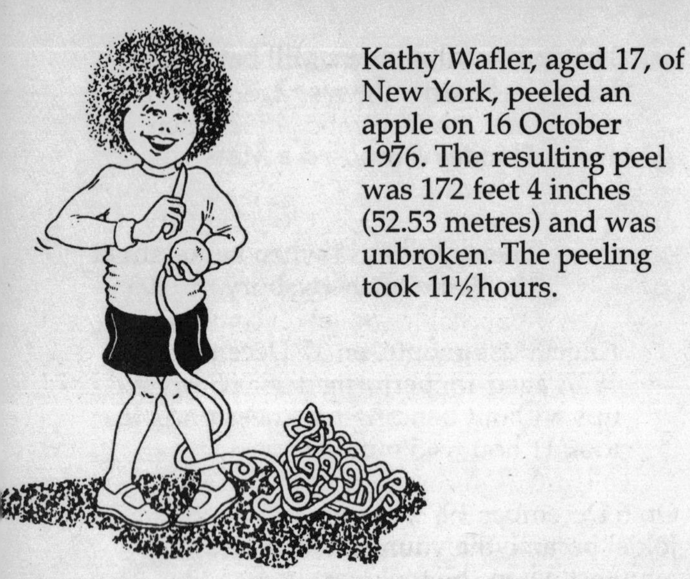

Kathy Wafler, aged 17, of New York, peeled an apple on 16 October 1976. The resulting peel was 172 feet 4 inches (52.53 metres) and was unbroken. The peeling took 11½ hours.

Pupils of East High School, Salt Lake City, USA, played a game of Musical Chairs in 1977 in which 1,789 people took part.

Joseph Henry Nuxhall began his baseball career in Cincinnati, USA, when aged 15 years 10 months, making him the youngest major league player of all time.

Schoolchildren from Hanover High School, Hanover, USA, leapfrogged for 555 miles (893 km) in 148 hours between 4 and 10 June 1977.

HRH Prince Albert Edward, later to become Edward VII, was made Prince of Wales on 8th December 1841 when he was 29 days old.

Octavio Guillen of Mexico City got engaged in 1902 when he was 15. There is nothing very remarkable in that, except that the engagement lasted 67 years and the couple finally married in June 1969.

Gertrude Ederle, aged 12 years 298 days, broke the world record for the 880 yards (800 metres) women's freestyle swimming in a total of 13 minutes 19.0 seconds in August 1919.

The 4 year old son of Henry IV of France married Françoise de Lorraine, who was 1 year younger than he.

Jane Aitchison of Reigate, Surrey, wrote a story called *The Pirates' Tale* when aged 5½. It was published by Penguin Books when she was 6½.

King George IV became a peer when he was seven years old.

Andrew Fitzgibbon, born in India on 13th May 1845, received a Victoria Cross medal for bravery on 21 August 1860 when aged 15 years 100 days.

On 9 March 1978, a teenager called Pat Donahue of Victoria, British Columbia, ate 91 pickled onions in 1 minute 8 seconds.

On 26 July 1966, Brenda Sherratt of West Bollington, Cheshire, when aged 18, became the first person to swim the full length of Loch Ness. She completed the 22¾ miles (36.6 km) in 31 hours 27 minutes.

Scotland's youngest Queen, Mary, was born on 8 December 1542. She acceded to the throne on 14 December 1542, when she was 6 days old.

A Monsieur Lolito of France ate a complete bicycle in 15 days, between 17 March and 2 April 1977. This is not a record anyone should try to beat!

Jan Bunford, born 26 July 1895 at Northfield, West Midlands, measured 6 feet 6 inches (1.98 metres) in height at the age of 13.

Between 29 July and 12 August 1978, Arron Marshall of Rockingham Park, Western Australia, took a shower that lasted 336 hours.

On 3 June 1961, Mrs Saadet Cor gave birth to a baby boy that weighed 24 lb 4 oz (11 kilograms).

A Norwegian boy, Roger Arntzen, in an accident in 1962, had a three hour heart stoppage and lived.

On 14 October 1967, a Turkish teenager called Mehemed Ali Halici recited 6,666 verses of the Koran from memory. It took 6 hours.

General Tom Thumb (real name Charles Stratton), born on 11 January 1838, was only 30½ inches tall (77.47 cm) when he was 12 years old.

Carolyn Webb of New South Wales, Australia, claims to be able to write backwards and upside-down, whilst blindfolded, with both hands and feet at the same time, writing that can be clearly read when looked at in a mirror.

When he was 10 years old, Robert Wadlow was 6 feet 5 inches (1.96 metres).

On 9 February 1980, Lang Martin of North Carolina, USA, balanced 7 golf balls on top of each other.

Du Val Senior High School Band of Maryland, USA, played for 100 hours 2 minutes, 13–17 May 1977.

Anthony Michael Kinch was born in County Wicklow, Ireland, on 13 June 1950, weighing 17 lb 3 oz (7.80 kilograms), making him the heaviest baby born in Ireland.

On 26 March 1980, 3000 children aged 3–9 took part a monster egg hunt in Georgia, USA, when 20,160 hardboiled eggs were hidden by the Air Patrol in the meadow of Stone Mountain Park.

14 year old Martina Ehlers of Ulm, Germany, on 20 September 1980, shelled 12 hardboiled eggs in 1 minute 59 seconds.

On 31 July 1980, 10 year old Adam Cook on holiday in Scotland skimmed a flat pebble across the calm surface of Loch Ness an estimated distance of 25 metres (82 feet).

On 5 April 1943, 19 year old Poon Lim of Hong Kong was rescued after being shipwrecked, having spent 133 days on a raft.

Probably the largest orchestra in the world was at a meeting of School Brass Bands in Norway, in August 1958, in which there were 12,600 players.

On 27 April 1980, a game of musical chairs was played at Ohio State University, USA, with 4378 students taking part.

On 24 March 1979, William Hallingsworth of New York, USA, walked 18 miles 880 yards (29.77 km) whilst balancing a full pint of milk on his head.

Miss Dawn Lee was born in Honolulu, Hawaii, USA, in February 1967. Her middle name is

Napuamahalaonaonekawe hiwehionakuahiweanena wawakehoonkakehoaale keeaonanainana-niakeao 'Hawaiikawao.

On 23 February 1952, at a hospital in Indianapolis, USA, a baby boy was born weighing 6 oz (170 grams). He was only 6½ inches (16.5 cm) long.

In July 1970, Michael Potter of Sittingbourne in Kent walked non-stop for 66½ hours covering 185 miles (298 km).

A group of ten youngsters from Aldbourne Methodist Youth Club from Wiltshire wheeled a hospital bed 411 miles (661 km) between 1 and 6 August 1970.

Florinda Zacchini in the 1940s used to be shot out of a cannon at 54 miles (87 km) per hour. On 17 August 1978, Miss Sue Evans aged 17 repeated the feat and was found to be 9.5 mm (0.37 inches) shorter when she landed.

On 12 November 1970, a total of 103 students from Bournemouth College crammed into a small Volkswagen car, their collective weight being over 6 tons (6096 kilograms). The car was then driven for 5 metres (16½ feet).

17 year old Brian Latasa foolishly touched an ultra-high-voltage power cable on 9 November 1967, and received a shock of 230,000 volts. He could easily have been killed, but fortunately he lived – creating a world record, having received the highest voltage electric shock. **DO NOT ATTEMPT TO BEAT THIS RECORD.**

On 8 September 1978, James Warbeck of Quebec built a card house that was 11 feet 7 inches high (3.53 metres) using 3,650 cards.

Gordon MacDonald, born 18 April 1971, listened to a record by Pink Floyd continuously through headphones for 27 hours 14 minutes when aged 9 years.

Between 20 and 28 July 1978, David Hathaway of Indiana, USA, played his guitar for 200 hours 2 minutes.

In March 1981, Robert Buchanon, aged 14, of Welwyn Garden City, ate 22 apples in 4 minutes 8.6 seconds.

On 30 August 1978, John Kirkland of Dallas, Texas, threw a plastic Frisbee 444 feet (135 metres).

Miss Alison Brown of Castle Douglas, Kircudbright, balanced a ping-pong ball on her nose for 2 hours 27 minutes on 5 April 1980, when aged 4 years 119 days.

In 1968, a Spanish boy called Zolilio Diaz rolled a hoop 600 miles (965 km) in 18 days.

Between 25 and 31 May 1980, five young St. John's Ambulance Cadets from Swansea gave a dummy the 'Kiss of Life' for 150 hours with 158,695 inflations.

With parents who both worked on a passenger cruise ship, by the time he was 6 years old Patrick Bond had spent two thirds of his life at sea.

On 19 August 1977, Emma Disley, born 17 May 1965, walked up Mount Snowdon in North Wales, (3560 feet/1085 metres) on stilts in 4 hours 5 minutes 45 seconds.

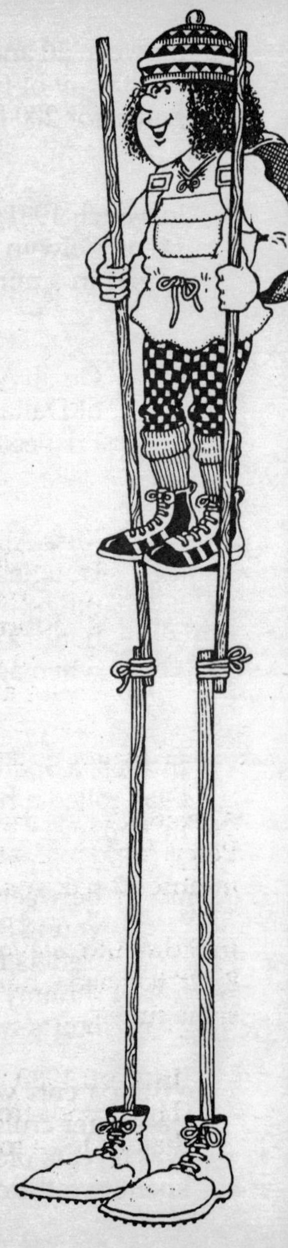

Sir Charles Brandon, aged 13 or 14, became Duke of Suffolk on 14 July, 1551. Unfortunately, he died of a fatal illness 30 minutes later.

Child film actor Jackie Coogan, who appeared in early Charlie Chaplin films, had earned a million dollars by 1920. He was born on 26 October 1914.

In the year 2310 BC, Pepi II became Pharaoh of Egypt aged 6 years.

Doreen Ashburnham-Ruffner was awarded the George Cross Medal in 1916 when she was 11 years old.

On 7 October 1979, Christopher Riggio of San Francisco, California, ran 28.5 miles (45.86 km) in an egg and spoon race using a fresh egg and a dessert spoon. He took 4 hours 34 minutes.

Alexandra Cawthera, aged 18, of Bolton Percy, Yorkshire, ate 23 raw eggs in 1 minute 22 seconds.

In Sidmouth, Devon, on 25 August 1978, 8,128 teenagers danced the Conga at the same time.

In April 1980, girls of the Havant Hurricanes from Hampshire twirled batons for a total of 55 hours.

At the age of 10, Peter Cartwright, born 1 March 1969, sat at the top of a set of step-ladders for 36 hours 11 minutes.

On 28 November 1980, 14 year old Peter Weston of Westbury-on-Trym, Bristol, read six plays by William Shakespeare aloud in 8 hours 47 minutes.

Rena Clark and Jeff Block at Frontier Village Armusement Park, California, between 1 July and 7 August 1978, rode a Big Wheel for 37 days.

On 17 July 1976, 17 year old Carol Douwe of Illinois, USA, ate 39 toffee apples in 34 minutes 58 seconds.

In June 1977, young Carl Burrows from Nottingham stood on one leg for 19 hours without any support.

In 1435, Henry Long (1420–1490) was elected Member of Parliament for Old Sarum at the age of 15.

On 1 July 1980, William Arthur Bryant, aged 17, balanced a fresh egg on his index finger for 7 minutes 42 seconds without dropping it.

When he was 11 years old, Robert Wadlow was 6 feet 7 inches (2 metres).

On 29 August 1980, at the age of 9, Fiona Timmis of Missouri, USA, bounced a ball continuously with her right hand for 5 hours 7 minutes.

On 3 January 1978, Eric Apilla of Mexico, aged 12 years, walked backwards for a distance of 27 miles (43.4 km) in 6 hours 16 minutes.

In 1968, an Australian teenager called Bill Irby threw 4002 hoops on to 4002 pegs in succession.

On 26 January 1981, 9 year old Gavin Beale of Whitehaven, Cumbria, juggled three apples continuously for 3 hours 14 minutes without dropping them.

French born André Furneaux, when aged 12, joined together 2,002 safety pins to make a chain approximately 190 feet (58 metres) long.

On 29 February 1904, Charles Wolfe was born in Hamburg, Germany. The surname 'Wolfe' is merely an abbreviation of his name which actually contains 590 letters.

In June of 1980, Emma Harwood, aged 8, made a daisy chain that consisted of 956 daisies.

In 28 days, at the age of 11, Sally Ann Jarvis knitted a scarf that was 62 feet long (18.9 metres) and 5 inches wide (15.24 cm), completing it on 19 May 1980.

The song most frequently sung by children is 'Happy Birthday To You'.

Patricia Reay, aged 12, caught a cold on 15 October 1979 and continued sneezing for a further 194 days. Some of the sneezes were at a force of 103.6 miles (166.7 km) per hour.

In the year 1900, one Johann Hurlinger of Austria walked 871 miles from Vienna to Paris, on his hands.

On 6 August 1941, Elaine Esponito of Florida, USA, went into an unconscious state after a serious operation when she was 6 years old. She remained in that state for 36 years 111 days.

Ralph and Carolyn Cummins of Clintwood, Virginia, USA, had five children. Catherine was born 20 February 1952, Carol, 20 February 1953, Charles, 20 February 1956, Claudia, 20 February 1961, and Cecilia, 20 February 1966. The chances of this happening are 1 in 17,797, 577, 730.

Pauline Musters, known as 'Princess Pauline', at the age of 9, in 1885, stood 21½ inches (55 cm) tall and weighed 3.31 pounds (1.5 kilograms).

Vegard Slettmoen in February 1974, aged 5, fell through some ice into a Norwegian river. He was not found for another 40 minutes, when he was discovered 8 feet (2.44 metres) under the water. Miraculously he survived suffering no ill effects.

On 21 July 1980, Peter Dowdeswell in Paris ate 144 prunes in 53.3 seconds.

On 6 February 1952, HRH Prince Charles, then aged 3, became Duke of Cornwall and eligible to sit in the House of Lords.

Matthew Russell Day, born on New Year's Day 1973, made his stage debut in a production of *Fiddler on the Roof* at the Regent Theatre, Chelmsford, on March 26 1973, aged 85 days.

On 24 August 1979, 16 year old Bruce McConachy of West Vancouver balanced 170 Canadian coins on top of a Canadian commemorative penny which was standing vertically on another coin.

William Frederick Price was enlisted into the army at the age of 11 years 356 days, in May 1903.

Actor Richard Hearne (1909–77) played a baby in a play at the age of 6 weeks and continued in the profession throughout his childhood and then on until his death.

On 15 June 1980, at the Yorkshire Television Studios, Joanne Brown aged 14 of Sheffield, achieved 113 decibels, beating all previous world records for the loudest voice.

In May 1969, a group yo-yo marathon record was achieved by six students from Leicester, when they kept three yo-yos on the go for 76 hours.

In 1968, a boy called Kelly Stanley of Queensland, Australia, climbed a 90 feet (27.43 metres) pine tree in 36 seconds.

In February 1957, Francine Pary, aged 17, of Toulouse, France, walked on a tightrope 50 feet (15.24 metres) in the air for 34 hours 15 minutes.

On 11 November 1970, young Bret Edmonds completed 125 hours 3 minutes in a rocking chair in Bath Abbey, Avon.

In December 1959, David Turner and David Such, of Twyford and Rushcombe Youth Club, remained on a see-saw for 80 hours without leaving.

On 12 January 1963, it was reported that in Russia a girl, Rosa Kuleshova, when completely blindfolded could identify colours by touch.

On 18 July 1980, 8 year old Arden Chapman of Louisiana, USA, caught a grape in his mouth that was thrown at him from a distance of 319 feet (97.23 metres).

On 26 September 1979, at the age of 14, Barry Littlemore of Dunblane, Scotland, balanced a 1p coin on his nose, without adhesive, for 2 hours 26 minutes 14 seconds.

When he was 12 years old, Robert Wadlow was 6 feet 10½ inches (2.09 metres).

Oscar Duval, born in New York, USA, 15 October 1965, drank 3 pints (1.7 litres) of milk in 2.56 seconds on 1 August 1980.

Terry Ratcliffe, aged 16, and Christina Woodcroft, aged 16, from 10.15 p.m. on 28 May to 2.13 p.m. on 30 May 1965, jived non-stop for 40 hours.

Between 15 and 30 November 1970, Peter Grooves, aged 19, of Basingstoke, Hampshire, acted as a disc-jockey for 360 hours.

On 15 August 1980, Maurice Brownlow aged 16, born in New Mexico, blew the yolks out of 24 fresh eggs in 9.56 minutes making only a pin prick in either end of each egg.

A paper aeroplane made by 11 year old Andrew Kiley of Nottingham was flown by him on 29 March 1981 a distance of 364 feet (111 metres).

Between 8 and 18 May 1980, Darlene Blume at Matraville Youth Club, Australia, bounced on a trampoline for 240 hours.

On 26 October 1953, J. P. Hughes of Melbourne, Australia, skipped without a break for 3 hours 10 minutes making 32, 809 turns.

In August 1978, while searching his garden in Shropshire with a metal detector, 12 year old Peter Barnes unearthed a Roman coin dating from the 1st century AD.

In 1891, Sylvaine Dornon walked for 1,830 miles (2944.5 km) on stilts taking 58 days.

On 29 June 1978, 11 year old hay fever sufferer Lesley Richard sneezed 61 times in 1 minute 57 seconds.

In an effort to help train a guide dog for the blind, 14 year old Belinda Haven and 15 year old Francis Langer collected 1200 silver milk bottle tops from friends and relations in just 15 days, in June 1977.

In January 1962, 10 year old Peter Byron of Harrogate started rolling a snowball in the snow until it had reached gigantic proportions. It was over 6½ feet (2 metres) in circumference and weighed an estimated half a ton.

Twins Susan and Sadie Jenkins, born 5 May 1968, when aged 12, in May 1980, took part in an experiment for thought projection. Although blindfolded, Sadie was able to tell which playing cards Susan had chosen from a pack of 52.

At Wakefield Youth Hostel, on 16 April 1971, John Wood ate 12 lemon quarters (3 lemons) in 162 seconds.

At the age of 15, on 1 February 1927, Amelia Finch sent a birthday card to her friend Paul Warburgh from her home in New Jersey, USA. They exchanged the same card for over 50 years!

In June 1978, Stephen Murrell of Crown Woods School, Eltham, Kent, passed 8 'A' levels at one sitting, 7 of them were grade 'A'.

Jeremy Powell and Gilbert Harris, both aged 15, living in adjoining houses, spoke to each other on the telephone for 50 consecutive hours between 9–12 June 1980.

In just 8 hours, on 3 September 1980, 17 year old Diana Wilson from Dunblane, Perthshire, knitted 2 cardigans, 2 pairs of socks, and 1 pair of gloves.

Kelly Liddiard of Oklahoma, USA, lived on the roof of her home for 10 days, from 13 to 22 March 1978, when aged 15 years 7 months.

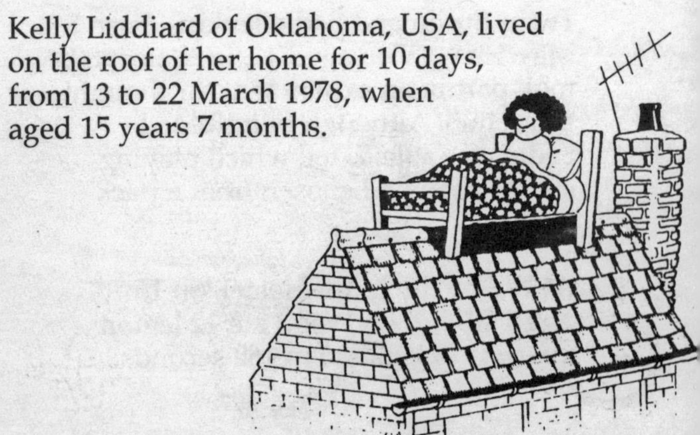

On 12 May 1977, Margot Ashford from Salisbury, aged 14 years 8 months, knitted 50 pairs of baby-bootees in 3 hours 4 minutes.

Barbara Jane Ellis of Bexhill-on-Sea, Sussex, at the age of 17, in April 1981, held the distinction of being able to write 160 words a minute in shorthand.

From 11 October to 24 November 1970, James Crowley Jnr. played the piano 22 hours daily for the 45 days, playing a total of 1,008 hours.

On 30 March 1979, 18 year old Christopher Hall achieved a speed of 60 miles per hour (96.5 km) on a home-made go-cart with four pram wheels.

FRAGILE

When he was 13 years old, Robert Wadlow was 7 feet 1¾ inches (2.18 metres).

On 24 July 1969, Michael George of Heaton Norris, Cheshire, completed 195 hours 17 minutes of piano playing.

In 1964, Gwendoline Beasley of Stretham, Cambridgeshire, aged 18, hiccupped continuously for a total of 64 days.

Malcolm Rossiter, aged 17, of Salisbury, Rhodesia, on 5 December 1963, built a tower from playing cards that was 22 storeys high.

On 23 April 1971, ten students from Dundee University, Scotland, played hopscotch for 125 hours.

In the Autumn of 1970, Bob Burwell of Queensland, Australia, threw a 6 oz (170 grams) boomerang 90 yards (82.3 metres).

At the age of 15, Delores Ann Johnson of Louisiana, USA, born in August 1946, was 6 feet 10 inches (2.03 metres) tall.

King Louis XIV of France ascended the throne on 14 May 1643, aged 4 years 231 days.

In 1933 the De Witt Clinton High School, in New York, USA, had 12,000 pupils.

On 25 September 1980, Simon Bravell of Penge, London, aged 16 years 273 days, successfully balanced 12 pint bottles of milk on top of each other without any breakages.

Vanessa Chalmers was born on 6 October 1970. Just before her 10th birthday in October 1980 she spent 3 hours 2 minutes 10 seconds pretending she was the speaking clock by saying the time every 10 seconds.

Peter Fordozi of New Jersey, USA, when aged 9 years, balanced a baseball on his head for 2 hours 19 minutes, on 14 September 1979.

4 days before his 18th birthday, motor enthusiast Barry Anderson assembled a car engine in 1 hour 14 minutes on 30 September 1980.

On 16 April 1980, the occasion of her 10th birthday, Pamela Jane Coverson of High Wycombe played the whole of Chopin's *Revolutionary Concerto* before an audience of 85 people, without playing a single wrong note.

On 25 August 1975, a junior team of eight, (average age 15 years 7 months) from Sir Thomas Rich's school, Gloucester, rowed the length of Loch Ness, 22.7 miles (35.5 km), in 2 hours 35 minutes 38.2 seconds.

The world record for carrying the most marbles in one pocket went to 9 year old Kevin Underwood of Knutsford, Cheshire, in August 1980, when he managed to fit 113 marbles into an ordinary trouser pocket.

Between 1 and 4 February 1979, two American teenagers, Pat Purcell and John McGlynn, completed 81 hours 12 minutes of alpine skiing.

Barbara Jones was born in the United States on 26 March 1937. At the 1952 Olympic Games in Helsinki, at the age of 15 years 123 days, she became the youngest winner of a gold medal for athletics.

Micha Magorri, born in Sicily in June 1969, sat on a garden swing for 8 hours 47 minutes on 30 August 1978.

The most brothers and sisters that any boy or girl has ever had is 67. Madame Vassilet of Russia (1816–1872) gave birth to a total of 68 children!

Margaret Johnson of Ohio, born 2 February 1970, at the age of 8, wore size 5 adult shoes.

Between 27 July and 3 August 1969, two blind teenagers, Michael Howell and Graham Roberts, travelled a distance of 8,098 miles by British Rail with a weekly roving ticket.

In May 1976, Jacqueline Jones of Texas, USA, completed a letter to her sister which took eight months to write and contained 1,113,747 words.

On 27 March 1977, a South African boy called David Haynes, aged 14 years 6 months, discovered an unknown species of millipede with 340 pairs of legs.

In 1980, pupils of Chosen Hill School, Gloucestershire, grew a tomato plant that measured 31 feet 6 inches in length (9.60 metres).

In March 1981, two unnamed pupils from Bolton Percy, Yorkshire, carried two buckets of water in relay over a distance of 5 miles (8.05 km) in 1 hour 46 minutes 17 seconds.

Peter Oakham, born 19 March 1968, is lucky enough to own one of the rarest dogs in the world, a Portuguese water dog (Cao de Agua).

At the age of 6 years, Amanda Ling, born 13 April 1942, had reached her fully grown adult height of 5 feet 2½ inches (1.59 metres).

In 1977, at the age of 15 years 316 days, Ross Hepburn became the youngest international athletics champion in the world.

On 19 December 1882, the daughter of Arthur Pepper of West Derby, Lancashire, was christened Ann Bertha Cecelia Diana Emily Fanny Gertrude Hypatia Inez Jane Kate Louisa Maud Nora Ophelia Quince Rebecca Starkey Teresa Ulysis Venus Winifred Xenophen Yetty Zeus Pepper.

From 20 December 1970 to 2 January 1971, young Feardorcha Aogain walked the complete length of Ireland, some 370 miles (595 km), in 13 days 5 hours.

Norman Darwood, who was born in 1918 and left school at the age of 14, he has had a total of 136 different jobs.

Gary Horton of Maidenhead was born on 19 June 1965. At the age of 15, in June 1980, he completed his newspaper round, a delivery of 300 papers, in 1 hour 3 minutes – entirely on foot.

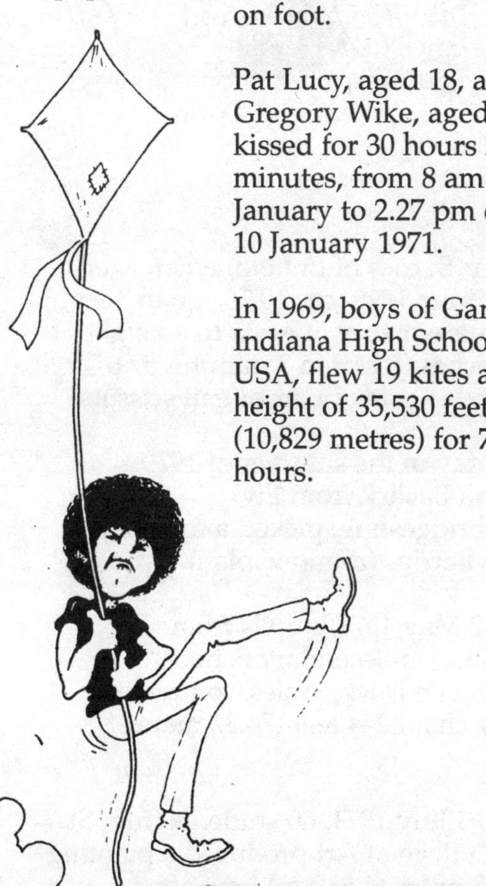

Pat Lucy, aged 18, and Gregory Wike, aged 19, kissed for 30 hours 27 minutes, from 8 am on 9 January to 2.27 pm on 10 January 1971.

In 1969, boys of Gary Indiana High School, USA, flew 19 kites at a height of 35,530 feet (10,829 metres) for 7 hours.

Trevor Barnes of Enfield, when aged 14 in June 1979, cut 10.76 square feet (1 square metre) of grass to a height of 2.4 inches (6 cm) in 3 minutes 57.6 seconds – with a pair of nail scissors!

One day in the summer of 1979, Gillian Baslick from Ely, Cambridgeshire, picked a total of 93 strawberries from one plant.

On 12 May 1971, pupils from Coronation Secondary School, Pembroke Dock, Wales, completed a daisy chain 244 feet (74.37 metres) long.

From 1 to 3 July 1971, 60 students from St. Alban's College of Art produced a painting that was 3 miles (4.83 km) long after painting non-stop for 60 hours.

In 1966, Philippa Smith in Woodborough, Nottinghamshire, found a 10-leaf clover.

On 18 August 1969, David Ryder, a victim of polio, from Chigwell, Essex, walked to Land's End from John O'Groats on crutches.

Leonore Modell of California, USA, swam the English Channel in 15 hours 33 minutes on 3 September 1964, when aged 14 years 5 months.

On 5 to 6 August 1979, Marcus Hooper of Eltham, Kent, swam the English Channel in 14 hours 37 minutes aged 12 years 53 days.

On 26 July 1979, at the age of 17, chess fanatic Stephen Dewson of London, successfully reached checkmate in 12 moves taking a record 4 minutes 9 seconds.

On 25 August 1978, Peter Dowdeswell of Earl's Barton, Northants, ate 3 lbs (1.36 kilograms) of potatoes in 1 minute 2 seconds.

Julie Wilkinson, born October 1968, found a total of 37 pips in one tangerine on 22 December 1980.

On 30 April 1981, 4 year old Emma Barrington rode 1½ miles (2.4 km) on the back of Boris, a pet St. Bernard dog, under the guidance of her parents.

In August 1979, 3 year old Poppy Mansfield of Los Angeles, USA, unintentionally created a world record by playing with her parents' telephone. Having accidentally obtained a number in Western Australia she ran up a bill for $5000.

On 17 June 1980, aged 13 years 29 days, Peter Hardcastle of Hamilton, New Zealand, remained in a bath for 17 hours 43 minutes – by which time the water was cold!

Michael Bryers of Milford Haven is reported to have caught an unknown species of fish weighing 256 lbs (116 kilograms) in June 1972, when he was 14 years old.

In May 1969, Paul Tully of Brisbane, Australia, ate thirty 2 ounce (56.7 grams) bags of potato crisps without a drink in 24 minutes 33.6 seconds.

On 6 October 1979, 12 year old Errol Bird of Lisburn, Ireland, yodelled for 10 hours 15 minutes.

On a particularly hot day in August 1976, Andrew Burrows of Ewell, Surrey, aged 12, successfully swatted 57 flies in 4 minutes 33 seconds.

It is reported that in 1808, an un-named 7 year old girl was executed for a crime in England. Since 1887, no person under the age of 18 has been executed and the death penalty was abolished in December 1969.

Marion Foster, aged 15, at her home in Monmouth, made 70 pancakes on 3 March 1981, Shrove Tuesday.

At the age of 16, Emma Read, from Highgate, London, was editor of her very own poetry magazine, becoming one of the world's youngest editors.

On 29 March 1979, super-sucker Philip Green of Newport, using an ordinary drinking straw, sucked 1 pint of milk in 31 seconds.

On 5 October 1978, Peter Dowdeswell of Northampton consumed 22 meat pies (each weighing 156 gm) in 18 minutes 13 seconds.

At Queen Elizabeth's Grammar School, Horncastle, four pupils, Christopher Berry, Stephen Crilley, Christopher Southall and Gary Wemyss played badminton for 60 hours 36 minutes between 26 and 28 August 1979.

In a basketball tournament in Stockholm, Sweden, Mats Wermelin, aged 13, scored all 272 points in a 272–0 win on February 1974.

18 year old David Taylor of Truro, Cornwall, in a drum marathon, played the tympani for 19 hours 22 minutes on 16 December 1977.

On 11 April 1972, an un-named boy from Kentucky walked barefoot non-stop for a distance of 32.3 miles (52 kilometres).

In July 1980, Samuel Wiley, aged 15 years 2 months, at his home in Florida, floated on an air bed in a swimming pool for 27 hours 47 minutes.

On 22 April 1979, two girls from Ramsgate in Kent, Amanda Turner, aged 13, and Julie King, aged 12, ran a 100 metre 3-legged race in 1.6 minutes.

George Bull, aged 19 of Chippenham, Wiltshire, ran 100 yards (91.44 metres) in 11.0 seconds on 26 October 1954. George was blind.

Ninion Jameson Finlay (born 1858) and Charles Reid (born 1864) were both 17 years 36 days old when they played Rugby Football for Scotland v. England, in 1875 and 1881 respectively.

On 4 February 1972, Colin Peter Beavan, aged 14 years 3 months, threw an ordinary football, with 2 hands, a distance of 173 yards (158 metres).

By August 1979, 8 year old Linda Baumman of Roswell, New Mexico, could speak fluently in six languages.

In October 1970, teenager Robert Sturgill of Aberdeen, Washington, USA, set a world drumming record of 150 hours.

Brian Trovell and Bruce Murray, both aged 13, once spent 18 hours in a New York departmental store elevator, travelling up to the 10th floor and down again.

In 1976, young Christopher Hudson of Hove, East Sussex, owned a snail from Sierra Leone that weighed 1 lb 7 oz (652 grams) and was 13½ inches (34.3 cm) from nose to tail.

On 4 January 1977, 25 students from the Bronx, New York, finished making a rag doll that was 23 feet (7 metres) long.

In 1745, when he was 6, Jozef Boruwalaski stood 17 inches tall (43.18 cm).

The country with the smallest number of children is the independent state of the Vatican City, Rome, which has a zero birth rate.

When he was 15 years old, Robert Wadlow was 7 feet 8 inches (2.34 metres).

Polly Gadsby, born 1837, began work in a company's packing department at the age of 9. She remained with the company for 86 years until her death at the age of 95.

In 1941, during the Second World War, 15 year old Private Patterson of Risca, Gwent, drove a 5-ton truck.

At Cebu City, in the Philippines, on April 24, 1968, Clark Palaez flew a Piper Tri-Pacer plane solo. He was aged 10 years 3 months.

On 27 April 1980, Brian Markham of Ohio, USA, when aged 13 years 112 days, played an electric organ for 23 hours 17 minutes.

On 4 March 1959, Maurie Rose Kirby, aged 17, completed 211 days 9 hours squatting on top of a 71 foot (21.6 metres) tall pole at Indianapolis, USA.

In 1740, at the age of 1, the celebrated midget 'Count' Josef Boruwalaski was 14 inches (26 cm) high.

On 15 August 1980, Davina O'Donnell of County Antrim, aged 16, threw a freshly laid hen's egg a distance of 301¾ feet (92 metres) without breaking the shell.

On 4 December 1980, 11 year old Simon Hawthorne of Grimsby made 1 toffee remain in his mouth for 1 hour 42 minutes.

Merril Wolf, born 28 August 1931, achieved his Bachelor of Arts degree in Music fromYale University, aged 14 years, in September 1945.

In the 1930s, Wilma Williams' parents were travelling entertainers. And everywhere her parents went Wilma went too. In the course of her travels young Wilma attended 265 different schools!

Between March 7 and 9 1977, teenager Norman English of Weston-Super-Mare played an electric accordion for 54 hours 1 minute.

From 9 to 13 July 1976, four pupils from Churchill School, Salisbury, Rhodesia (now Zimbabwe), played the bagpipes for 100 consecutive hours.

Marlene Raymond, aged 15, on 24 June 1973, limbo danced under a flaming bar that was just 6⅛ inches (15.56 cm) off the floor.

On 19 June 1978, Graeme Hurry of Coventry completed 4 years of sleeping outside in a tent.

On 8 February 1974, David Donaghue and John Cartwright dropped a fresh egg 600 feet (182.9 metres) from a helicopter without it breaking.

From 20 August to 2 September 1976, teenagers Gary Mandau, Chris Lyons and Dana Dover in Oregon, USA, rode on a merry-go-round for 312 hours 43 minutes.

Between 13 and 18 July 1978, teenagers James Bruse and Richard Rodrigues covered 1,805 miles (2,904 km) on a roller coaster in 124 hours.

On 3 October 1976, Jo Ann Barnes, aged 15, hula hooped with 62 hoops.

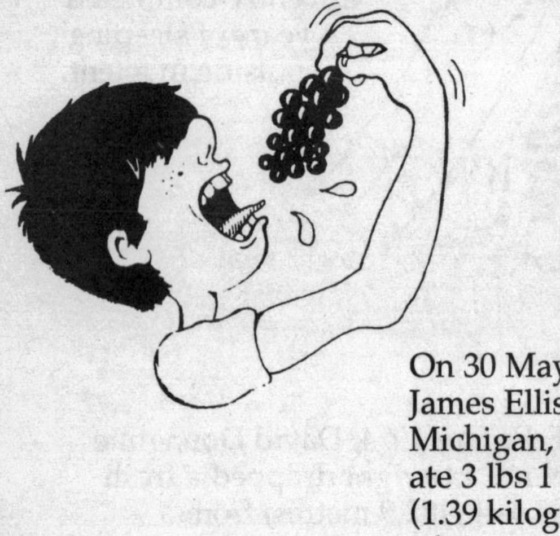

On 30 May 1976, James Ellis of Michigan, USA, ate 3 lbs 1 oz (1.39 kilograms) of grapes in 34.6 seconds.

From 26 to 28 June 1975, five 'majorettes' from Portland High School, Maine, USA, twirled their batons for a total of 44 hours.

In 1972, Roy Woodward, a boy scout from London, tossed a pancake 2,105 times.

Two teams from Portishead Youth Club, Bristol, played 5-a-side football for 38 hours 5 minutes, ending at 10.15 am. on 15 November 1970.

Teenager Ian Beaton of Victoria, Australia, built a model boat in 18 months, using 41,000 matches.

A tabby cat named simply 'Cat', belonging to 12 year old Michael Wentworth, has had 203 kittens in all.

Calvin Phillips, born 14 January 1791, weighed 2 lb (907 grams) at birth and stopped growing at the age of 5. At 19 he was 26½ inches (67.3 cm) tall.

Jerrald and Jerraldine Paris, born in Louisville, Illinois, USA, both weighed exactly 11 lb (4.99 kilograms) when born, on 8 January 1941, making them the heaviest twins on record.

Graham Whitelaw, born 1960, played the longest organ recital on record at Glasgow University from 14 to 16 January 1970. The recital lasted 40 hours.

On 19 March 1980, 16 year old Rita Negus from Wednesbury talked non-stop for 9 hours 5 minutes.

In 1743, 12 year old Matthew Bartholomew of London, is said to have consumed 12 oysters in 15 seconds, complete with shells.

On 1 August 1971, in Washington, USA, teenagers Dale Stenson and Gerry Muns walked 32.9 miles (52.94 km), 3-legged, in 35 hours 39 minutes.

On 1 August 1971, James Anderson and Lyle Hendrikson remained on a swing for 100 hours at the Seattle Sea Fair, Washington, USA.

In March 1971, in a game of Monopoly which lasted 75½ hours, Kevin Daniel and Steven Skaggs 'served' 104 jail sentences.

Between 28 and 30 April 1971, eleven students from Leeds Polytechnic read aloud the complete works of Shakespeare in 53 hours 17 minutes.

Kevin Doyle, aged 16 years, having the burning ambition to be a male model, remained motionless for 3½ hours, in a standing position.

In July 1970, in the Jamma district of India, a school became the smallest in the world, with just one pupil and one teacher.

Jean Henderson and Joyce Ritter of New York, USA, were both born at the same time of day on 20 February 1947. They look like identical twins, but are not related in any way.

In 1977 Michael Hwan, 18 years old, walked from Singapore to London, a distance of 18,518 miles (29,800 km) in 81 weeks.

On 18 August 1980, Mary Jane Freeman of Illinois, USA, born 27 August 1965, skipped for 3 hours 10 minutes, turning the rope 32,809 times.

Between 7 and 9 September 1979, two 13 year olds, Fiona Brindley and Muriel Watson, sang non-stop for 28 hours 3 minutes.

On 31 October 1979, using an ordinary bicycle, Nigel Jefferson of Utah, USA, aged 14 years 3 months, remained stationary without any support for 4 hours 22 minutes.

In 1749, when he was 10, Jozef 'Count' Boruwalaski was 20¾ inches (53 cm) tall.

On 1 July 1979, 15 year old Peter Weston of Chatham, Kent, released a gas filled balloon with a card stating his name and address. The following day the balloon was discovered at Montdidier, France.

At the age of 17 years 180 days, Wilfredo Benitez, born 8 September 1958, became the youngest light-welterweight champion on 6 March 1976.

In July 1974, 17 year old Richard Anstey from Plymouth made a model of the aircraft carrier *Ark Royal* using 5,282 matchsticks.

On 1 August 1980, 9 year old Robin Mitford balanced 5 golf balls on top of each other.

In 1980, a wildlife conservationist, 16 year old Stephen Daniels of Norfolk, collected frogs-spawn from which he eventually bred 198 frogs.

In 1980, Noele Hayes from Pinner, Middlesex, aged 9, managed to suck an ordinary mint humbug sweet for 3 hours 7 minutes.

By 27 April 1981, science fiction fanatic Peter Wright of Stepney had seen the film *Star Wars* no less than 22 times.

On 25 August 1980, Stephen Clarke of Stonebridge Park, London, found 3 four-leaved clovers on a day trip to Blenheim.

In August 1980, 6 year old James Philips built 30 sandcastles in 35 minutes on the beach at Bournemouth, demolishing them all completely in 22 seconds.

The most common name in the world given to baby boys is Mohammed.

When aged 10 years old, Pico de la Mirandola knew Latin, Greek, Hebrew, Chaldee, and Arabic.

As a schoolboy, Thomas Chatterton (1752–1770) taught himself medieval English and used it to compose poems by an imaginary medieval monk, which deceived the literary world for over a century.

Peter the Great of Russia was said to be so strong as a child that he could break silver coins with his fingers.

Muscular Gavin Woodfield of Northampton, when aged 14 years 5 months, in July 1979, was able to lift a 50 lb (22.7 kilograms) weight above his head for 5 minutes.

On 14 July 1979, Peter Adamson, aged 17 years 7 months, walked a distance of 2½ miles (4.02 km) with 7 year old Linda Ecklor riding piggyback.

On 8 June 1980, 12 year old Nicola Westmacott of Tonbridge, Kent, bounced a tennis ball on a nylon stringed tennis racket for 98 minutes without once letting it touch the floor.

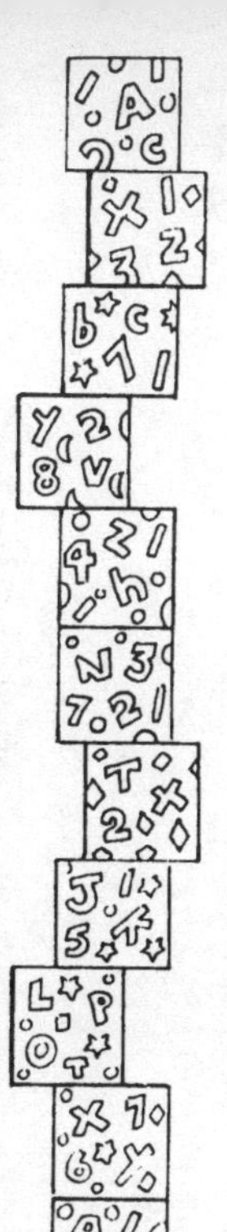

On 6 March 1961, Adam Norfolk, aged 9, from Whitehaven, Cumbria, whistled continuously for 3 hours 2 minutes.

James Weir (1819–1821) of Strathclyde, Scotland, weighed at the age of 13 months 8 stone (50.8 kilograms).

On 19 November 1979, 10 year old Daniel Errington built a single column of bricks, each 6 cm square, to a height of just over 9¾ feet (3 metres).

At the age of 13 months, James Weir, born in Strathclyde, Scotland, in 1819, was 3 ft 4 inches (1.01 metres) in height.

In 1979 Paul Wilson of New Zealand held the current record for the fastest time recorded while running backwards, running 110 yards (100 metres) in 14.4 seconds on 22 September.

From 9–10 August 1980, Peter Sabberton and Simon Cross, both aged 14, from Llandudno, North Wales, played table-tennis continuously for 8 hours 19 minutes.

Terence Miller, born 2 March 1932, at the age of 19 played football for Plaistow United, and scored the greatest number of goals by an individual in a home international, a record number of 11 when England defeated Wales 13–3 in 1951.

From 1965–1969, Karen Jenkins, born in Derby on 3 January 1960, set a record by not having one day's absence from school in 4 years.

Sandra McGeogh of Aberdeen, Scotland, at the age of 18, in September 1979, danced a Highland jig accompanied by bagpipes for 6 hours 46 minutes.

Sarah Griffin of Doncaster, Yorkshire, when aged 11 years, skipped using a standard skipping-rope, a distance of 82 feet (25 metres) in 1 minute 20 seconds on 2 October 1979.

At the age of 14, Shirley Campbell of Torquay, Devon, typed the numbers 'one, two, three, four . . .' and so on in words up to 'five thousand' over a period of 3 days, in February 1981.

Frances March, born 19 April 1967, from Liverpool, used an ordinary blue-ink biro pen at school for 3 years 6 months before it ran out.

On 15 October 1978, 13 year old Jenny Donstable of Whitby, Yorkshire, consumed 100 pieces of macaroni with a cocktail stick in 2 minutes 3 seconds.

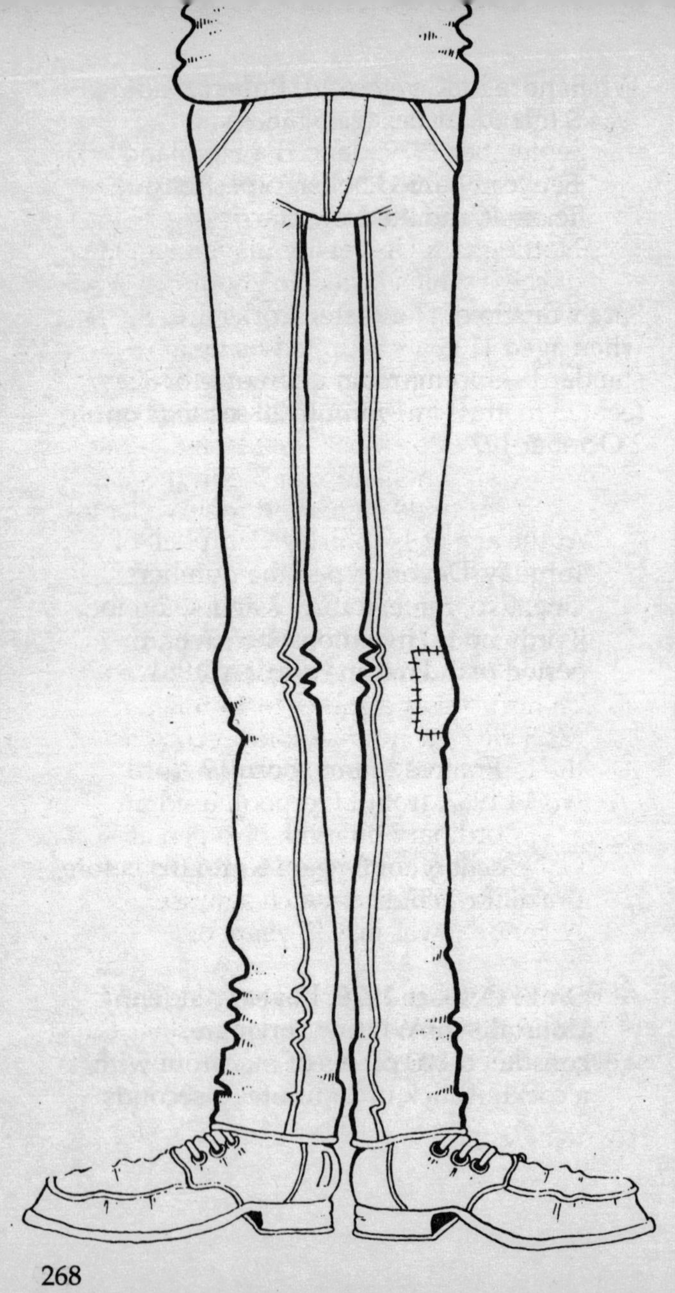

When he was 17 years old, Robert Wadlow was 8 feet 0½ inches (2.45 metres).

Between 6–13 October 1979, Philip Thomas and Andrew Harris of Nottingham University played a game of chess which lasted 165 hours 9 minutes.

Marina Embroden of Michigan, USA, aged 13 years 6 months, on 15 September 1980, managed to spin non-stop for 3 minutes 22 seconds on her left foot whilst ice skating.

On 16 November 1976, Kevin Tyerman of Hurleston High School, New South Wales, Australia, crawled on his knees a distance of 14 miles (22.5 km), creating a world record for the longest voluntary crawl in the world.

G. Dorval, who played football for Brazil, in 1957 in a match against Argentina, was just 15 years old.

At the age of 14, in 1978, Bosco Rosenfield of New York, USA, was receiving $1000 a week pocket money.

At Harrow, Middlesex, on 25 May 1971, John Wilson caught a fresh hen's egg thrown at him from a distance of 268 feet 7 inches (81.9 metres).

Millicent Barclay, born 10 July 1872, became eligible for a pension at birth owing to the death of her father a few months earlier. The pension was to continue until her marriage. She died unmarried aged 97 years 3 months having drawn the pension her entire life.

Gaston Pargano of Paris, France, aged 14 years 27 days, peeled 52 grapes in 6 minutes 48 seconds, on 27 May 1977.

Hillary Taylor, born 5 May 1962, when aged 17, in September 1979, played solo cello for 15 hours 30 minutes in aid of charity.

The last Sharifian Emperor of Morocco, who had more than one wife, was said to have been the father of 548 sons and 340 daughters – that is 888 children in all!

In 1642, Eliza Waller and Edward Longhorn both aged 2 years, were married in the parish of Ilchester.

At the time of her death on 1 March 1895, when she was 19 years old, renowned midget Pauline Musters was 23.2 inches (58.9 cm) tall.

Pamela Toynbee, aged 12 years, of Dunstable, had a pet snail which could move at a speed of 31 yards (28.3 metres) an hour.

While a boy, Barry Burke worked as a stagehand at the Palace Theatre, Fort Worth, Texas. He replaced a lightbulb on 21 September 1908. That bulb was still burning, over 70 years later. The average bulb lasts 750 hours.

In September 1967, Adam Thompson, aged 8 years, of Victoria, Australia, discovered an earthworm which measured 6½ feet (2 metres) in length. The longest earthworm on record, however, measured 22 feet (6.7 metres).

The famous artist Sir Edwin Landseer, best known for his paintings of dogs and horses, exhibited some of his work at the Royal Academy in 1815 when he was 13 years old.

On 4 May 1980, 10 year old Alison Wingard of Reading found an 8-leaved clover.

On 18 October 1974, Darrell Bronson, aged just 6 years old, recited the whole of *The Raven* by Edgar Allan Poe, a 108 line poem, from memory.

Spanish born Rosalia Cabanes of Madrid, aged 7 years, stood in an upright position without moving for 3 hours 15 minutes on 7 January 1978.

Iain Stinson and John Whiteley of Royal Holloway College, Surrey, on 6–9 February 1970, played the harmonium non-stop for a total of 72 hours.

In 1964, while in his garden, 8 year old Paul Cockerton of Essex unearthed a George I coin dated 1720, now over 250 years old.

Eight year old Maurice Winnard of Dover, whilst digging his garden on 11 May 1979, discovered a fossil estimated by experts to be 100,000,000 years old.

Twelve year old Bernard Malvoire of France coxed a boat to win a world title in the Olympic regatta in 1952, at Helsinki.

On 11 March 1979, 16 year old Paddy McMonagle, whilst fishing at Lough Eyes, Co. Fermanagh, caught a Rainbow Trout weighing 5 lbs 7 oz (2.47 km).

Major General Dudley Johnson VC received the Queen's South Africa Medal from Queen Victoria when he was 16 years old in 1900.

In October 1967, four members of St. Mary's Youth Club, Balham, London, stood in a circle and ate 100 yards (91.5 metres) of spaghetti in 1 minute 34 seconds.

On 19 March 1974, Martin John Elmsworth of New Biggington, aged 16, walked a distance of 1 mile (1.609 km) with his feet tied together.

Sir Temulji Nariman and Lady Nariman were married in India in 1853 when both were 5 years old.

On 13 March 1978, 18 year old Stephen Barkway completed building a boat 4.7 inches (12 cm) long inside a wine bottle. The task took him 4 months.

In 44 minutes, in October 1976, Chuck Addleman of Alberta, Canada, when aged 13 years, painted the frame of his bicycle with gold paint, without spilling one drop.

On 10 March 1967, in Mexico City, a mother had 8 babies, known as octuplets. The 4 boys were all called Jose and all the 4 girls Josefina.

Using a standard sheet for a double bed, 11 year old Paul Peterson of Blackpool, Lancs, in June 1977 (Jubilee Year), made one of the world's largest Union Jacks with the help of red and blue paint.

Between 20 and 22 August 1976, 12 year old Peter Northcott of Austin, Texas, USA, spent 28 hours in a hammock hung between 2 trees.

Wearing a pair of thick leather gloves for protection, 16 year old Malcolm Westward knocked 36 3 inch (7.62 cm) nails into a block of wood, in 1 minute 42 seconds.

In Autumn 1979, 9 year old Sally Gardner, on a visit to Epping Forest, Essex, collected 150 acorns in 19 minutes.

The day Margaret Gordon was born in Horsham, Sussex, on 5 August 1958, hailstones weighing 5 ounces (142 grams) each fell, the heaviest hailstones on record in the U.K.

A gerbil belonging to Heather James of High Wycombe, Bucks, gave birth to 11 babies on 4 May 1980 – a record number for a gerbil.

On a trampoline, under the guidance of gymnastic instructors, 14 year old Edward Langham of Colchester, Essex, performed 6 backward somersaults in 192 seconds, on 7 June 1980.

Wearing boxing gloves 15 year old Jonathan Buller of Leeds ate 42 peanuts in 1 minute 49 seconds.

The fastest shoe-lacer in the United Kingdom was 11 year old Drummond McGlynn of Edinburgh, Scotland, who could tie up his two shoe laces in 6 seconds.

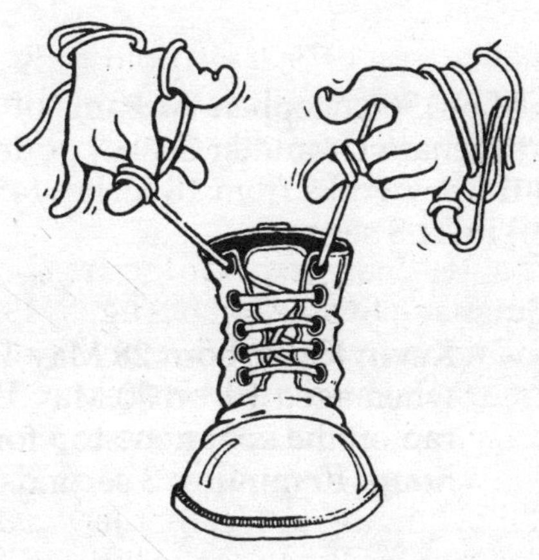

With both hands tied behind her back, 12 year old Beryl Cuthbertson wrote a 2-page letter, with a pencil between her teeth. She wrote 216 words, all clearly legible.

Between 4–9 August 1975, Norman Hazeldean, Alan Giles, Tom Barton and Keith Ollet of East Sussex played a game of Scrabble that lasted 120 hours.

Malaysian born Wan Si Wong, aged 9, can, it is claimed, read with her elbows whilst blindfolded.

In May 1966, Stephen Williams of Altrincham Grammar School potted 24 tiddleywinks from 18 inches (45 cm) in 21.8 seconds.

Kevin Kirby, born 28 May 1970, when aged 10, on 30 May 1980, ran on the spot non-stop for 3 hours 10 minutes 3 seconds.

Between 15–31 August 1979 Mark Kavanagh, Anthony Heywood, John Tierney and Graham Smith of St. Anselm's College, Birkenhead, played a game of Monopoly lasting 384 hours.

By mid-1980, postcard collector Ashley Copnall, aged 13, of Stroud, had in her scrapbooks 1517 postcards from over 30 different countries around the world.

The world record for the fastest dresser goes to 10 year old Jason Frost of Shanklin, Isle of Wight, who can dress himself in 1 minute 58 seconds, which involves putting on 9 separate garments, including shoes.

Exploring his grandmother's attic, 14 year old Nicholas Hayes of Gravesend discovered a very dusty vase. Having cleaned it up, the vase was later valued and sold at Sotheby's, London, for £2,600.

In 1858, a baby girl called Caroline was born. She had the longest known surname in the United Kingdom: Temple-Nugent-Chandos-Brydges-Grenville.

On 1 August 1980, Martin Hedges, aged 13, of Walton-Upon-Thames, managed to keep an ice-cube in his mouth 7 minutes 53 seconds before it melted completely.

Using her feet to propel her, 15 year old Deborah Twining of Bristol, Avon, swivelled round in her father's swivel chair non-stop for 1 hour 16 minutes on 19 November 1980.

The longest time anyone has been able to balance 2 marbles on their forehead, without adhesive, is 2 minutes 29 seconds, a record achieved by 11 year old Alexander Thompson on 30 December 1980.

Nicknamed 'Rip Van Winkle', 15 year old sleeper Marcus Bourne of Sidmouth, Devon, required 5 alarm clocks around his bed to rouse him each morning.

On 8 October 1977, ten teenagers from Victoria, Australia, picked 10,642 apples in 8 hours.

On 16 March 1980, 17 year old Margaret Bohann of Highgate, London, managed to successfully clip 52 haircurlers in her hair in under half an hour.

Between 28 March and 13 May 1977, George Partridge and Tamara Marquez of Auburn High School, Washington, USA, spent 1101 hours 40 minutes on an indoor seesaw.

On 19 September 1980, 15 year old Dale Kerry of Maryland, Baltimore, USA, played an electric guitar for 14 hours.

Between 24 and 27 October 1979, Richard Jacobs and Carlton Palmer of Lion Farm Scout Pack, Smethwick, South Midlands, performed the longest ever game of hopscotch. It lasted 70 hours.

On 11 June 1977, five teenagers aged 14–16 from Sydney, Australia, peeled 170 pounds (77.1 kilograms) of potatoes in 45 minutes.

In 1979, Dean Twyford of Ely, Cambridgeshire, born 14 May 1969, unearthed a carrot that weighed 3 lb 1 oz (1.38 kilograms).

Maralyn Avery, aged 19, of Folkestone, Kent, sat in a deckchair for 18 hours 3 minutes on 28 July 1978.

On 1 May 1981, Robert Hollingsworth, aged 12, of Woodford Green, London, tied 4 knots from the Boy Scout Handbook (Clove hitch, square knot, two half hitches, and a sheep bend) in 37 seconds.

17 year old Trevor Baxter, born 1 October 1962, of Burgess Hill, Sussex, holds the record for the highest skateboard jump of 5 feet 2 inches (1.575 metres) which he achieved in Glasgow at the UK Championships on 22 September 1979.

On 22 September 1978, Andrew Gleed of Ipswich caught 62 10 pence pieces flipped from his forearm to the palm of his hand.

One of the most conquering conkers in the world belongs to 14 year old Andrew Jenkinson of Poole, Dorset, who claims his conker is untreated and is a 'nine hundreder'.

Between 9 and 11 June 1972, Ronald Gisbey and Clifford Roach, both aged 14, rode a distance of 50 miles (80.5 km) on a tandem bicycle.

On 16 March 1972, 8 year old Simon Charnley managed to knock down 20 wooden skittles with one ball.

On 3 January 1962, 10 year old Geoffrey Sobers of Dumfries, Scotland, built a snowman that was exactly 2 metres in height.

In a Junior House cricket match, in June 1899, 13 year old Arthur Collins scored 628 not out in 6 hours 50 minutes over five afternoons' batting.

On 16 September 1969, Craig Jones in Pardeeville, Wisconsin, USA, spat a melon seed 33 feet 3½ inches (10.15 metres).

In November 1977, 3 year old Misty Lloyd, born 3 October 1974, could play 6 different tunes on the piano.

Linda Ellis, aged 15 years 2 days, on 6 June 1977 played the card game 'Patience' for 8 hours 31 minutes.

On 2 February 1971, 16 year old John Nichol at Reeds School, Cobham, Surrey, made the largest potato crisp in the world, measuring 5 inches by 3 inches (12.7 cm by 7.62 cm).

On 7 May 1977, 16 year old Adrian West of Oxford juggled successfully with 3 fresh eggs for 3 minutes 29 seconds, without any breakages.

The youngest actress ever to win an Oscar award was 6 year old Shirley Temple in 1934.

The largest Union Jack in the whole world measured 240 feet by 108 feet (73.15 x 32.91 m) and was made by Form 4Y of Bradley Rowe School, Exeter, in 1976.

On 1 September 1974, 13 year old Neil Gallow of Windsor had a chest measurement of 42 inches (106.7 cm).

On 14 December 1973, Michael Helliwell of Elland, York, aged 17, headed a ball 12,100 times in 54 minutes 22 seconds.

19 year old Simon Patterson swam from France to England, underwater, on 28 July 1962 in 14 hours 50 minutes.

SAY GOODBYE TO ROBERT WADLOW

When he was 19 years old, Robert Wadlow was 8 feet 5½ inches (2.58 metres). By the time he was 22, his height was 8 feet 11 inches (2.72 metres) and he was the tallest human being ever known.

Other fun titles available from Madcap Books

0 233 99320 7	Crazy Crosswords	£1.00
0 233 99318 5	Crazy Graffiti	£1.00
0 233 99316 9	Crazy Hoaxes	£1.00
0 233 99315 0	Crazy Howlers	£1.00
0 233 99098 4	Crazy Inventions	£1.00
0 233 99319 3	Crazy Riddles	£1.00
0 233 99063 1	Crazy Spy File	£1.00
0 233 99317 7	Crazy Tongue Twisters	£1.00
0 233 99097 6	Crazy Words	£1.00
0 233 99376 2	The Knockout Knock-Knock Joke Book	£2.99
0 233 99192 1	The Madcap Giant Book of Jokes	£2.99
0 233 99088 7	The Rotten Eggs Joke Book	£2.99
0 233 99089 5	The Teddy Bear Joke Book	£2.99
0 233 99062 3	A Trunk Full of Laughs	£2.99
0 233 99050 X	Bony Skeleton's Rib Ticker	£2.50
0 233 99051 8	St Dodger's School Yearbook	£3.50

All these books are available at your local bookshop or can be ordered direct from Littlehampton Book Services, 10-14 Eldon Way, Littlehampton, West Sussex, BN17 7HE. Tel: 01903 721596, fax: 01903 828802